RETHINKING FEAR

**A simple, unique approach
to reprogram old patterns
for a happier, more confident life**

Carol Rifon

CR Press   Cottonwood, Arizona

RETHINKING FEAR
A simple, unique approach
to reprogram old patterns
for a happier, more confident life

Dedication

To my husband, Charles Riggio

Special Thanks

To Andrea Hurst for consultation and guidance

To Geneva Agnos for production assistance

Table of Contents

FOREWORD

Having served the mental health field as a psychologist for over thirty years and a clinician for almost fifty years, I continuously search through readings and workshops for illuminating theories and practices. Although my clients have often confronted me with unique, and sometimes mysterious, conundrums, the human mind contains similar patterns with which all individuals struggle.

Over the years, my office bookcase has become overloaded with books; however, there are only a few volumes that stand out on the shelves. *Rethinking Fear* will sit with those few, but unique, volumes.

This is a valuable book containing the wisdom of internalized thought and feeling gained from the intertwining of the positive and negative experiences of life, and the achievement of knowledge from the various mental health professions. Specifically, *Rethinking Fear* grants readers the ability to empower themselves on both cognitive and emotional levels.

Utilizing the ideas and strategies of emotional intelligence, neuroscience, mindfulness, cognitive-behavior interventions and child-play stories, Ms. Rifon provides the reader the chance to access the implicit memory system and to move toward explicit cognitive realizations. In other words, the reader is able to access the roots of fear which may be linked to past traumatic life episodes. At the same time, the reader is given the opportunity to learn new tools to employ in future potentially anxious situations.

As I have done with other valued books, two copies of *Rethinking Fear* will be kept on my shelf. One copy containing yellow markings for my occasional review and one copy encompassing the worn pages from clients who have benefited from its treasures which have led them to an empowering sense over fear with renewed identity definition, clarified intention toward life purpose and overriding enjoyment in life's meaning.

Terry W. Moore, Ph.D.
Licensed Psychologist
Arizona #1098

PREFACE

One of my passions is providing individuals with tools to help them succeed. Another passion is my interest in the brain, especially as it relates to cognitive functioning and emotional intelligence.

For over 30 years, I have combined both of these passions in management, employee development, team building and personal responsibility training which I created and presented for individuals, businesses, colleges and the United States Navy.

This book addresses one of the most common issues I have seen deter individuals from moving forward in their lives and their careers - FEAR. Fear of failing. Fear of feeling. Fear of striving. Fear of speaking. Fear of trusting. Fear of trying. Fear of even the slightest change.

Neurological research (see note) has shown that chronic stress, such as fear, inhibits the brain's ability to regenerate neurons. This limits mental function needed to discover, learn, create and succeed in life.

Rethinking Fear was written to provide creative exercises that help stimulate cognitive, emotional and neurotransmitter functions to help individuals override fearful patterns and create happier lives.

The goal of this book is to provide you with tools to:
- better understand your fear
- increase your cognitive function and emotional intelligence to actively deal with your fear
- replace fearful patterns with freeing patterns

The more competent you feel about your coping skills, the less you will fear.

Note: For neurological research, check out www.sharpbrains.com. Alvaro Fernandez, CEO of this independent research firm, hosts international virtual summits of medical, science, research and technology professionals discussing the latest in neuroscience.

INTRODUCTION

How often have we hampered our careers, relationships or happiness due to fear? In my training over the past 30 years, I have seen fear hold back promising individuals again and again.

Rather than taking the time to rethink our fear, we quickly push fear away as if it were outside of us. The consequence we fear may be outside us, but our fear comes from within us. We often forget we have the power to create it, control it or conquer it.

Years ago, I was told a story about a twelve-year-old slave who repeatedly ran away. In an effort to control her, her captors chained one of her ankles to a post. Upon bringing her food, her friend chided her about the futility of running and being worse off now than before. The young girl answered, "They haven't won. They can never chain my mind. My mind can run away whenever it wants. I can think whatever I want whenever I want. They can't control me." How incredibly resilient that young girl's spirit! Even in the midst of insurmountable obstacles, she used her mind to her advantage.

There is a neurological reason that story remains with me. Simply speaking, when someone else's story impacts our emotions, our brain's limbic system (the complex structure in the brain primarily responsible for emotion and formation of memories) captures it and remembers. The words *your mind can think whatever it wants whenever it wants* could have been recited or read, but they would not have had the impact of that story.

Our brains are fascinating and flexible instruments. All day long, our brains are programmed and reprogrammed by our thoughts and actions. With each thought or action, neurotransmitters in our brains create chemical connections. These chemical connections are like bridges containing that thought or action. The next time we have a similar thought or action, our brain finds that existing bridge and reuses it. Repetition of the same thought or action shortens that bridge and eventually that thought or action becomes our "go to" way of behaving.

For example, by repeatedly thinking and acting from fear, our "go to bridge" becomes a fearful response. In order to create healthier "go to bridges" that will enable us to improve our lives, we need to rethink our fear.

So, how do we rethink fear?   We can start by accepting that fear is an emotion. Once we feel an emotion, we can do whatever we want with it. An emotion in and of itself is simply a feeling. What we choose to *do* with it helps us or hurts us.

Let's consider the following two scenarios:

- Scenario 1 – You are walking down the street and notice a safe falling out of the sky. You quickly assess that if it falls on your head, it may kill you. Your fear of possible death propels you to jump out of the way. Your logical conclusion that you could be killed by a falling safe allowed you to use the emotion fear to benefit you.

- Scenario 2 – You are afraid to leave your home for fear a safe will drop out of the sky, fall on your head and kill you. Your illogical fear of an event that has little probability of happening is allowing the emotion fear to control and diminish your freedom.

Our lives are made better or worse by how we handle our emotions. Neurological studies have shown that our ability to recognize and manage our emotions is critical for thriving in our fast-paced environment.

Every day, we encounter experiences in our lives. We often cannot control the experiences, but we have absolute power over how we respond to them. We can choose to be logical, illogical, hysterical, calm, open or closed. When we allow fear to make our choices, we **limit our freedom**.

We can use the power of our brains to rethink those fears. We can sweep away the old fears that are holding us back and clean out the fearful cobwebs. We can throw open the windows and allow illuminating insights to breeze through.   We can enthusiastically embrace opportunities for improving our lives.

The moment we explore a new thought our brains expand, generating new neurotransmitters. Imagine that! Take a moment to visualize it. Every new thought expands the neurons throughout our brains creating pathways to more confident and productive lives.

The chapters on the following pages use multi-dimensional stimuli to help you rethink your fear so you can better understand why you feel it and how you can resolve it.

The Emotional Intelligence chapter will help open your mind to the value of understanding your own and others emotions. It focuses on taking responsibility for your ABC's (Attitude, Behavior and Choices). The key message is **you cannot change anyone but yourself**. This is a significant point in creating happiness and achieving success in life. The sooner you learn it, the more freedom you will enjoy.

Each of the A to Z chapters begins with a sketch of the character in a scenario. The black and white sketch encourages your mind to creatively visualize the characters' movements as you read. Your creativity stimulates your neurons.

Each scenario addresses a common fear viewed through an anthropomorphic eye. This method of story-telling removes you from the fear element and allows you to emotionally connect with the character and cognitively examine the fear more safely. Opening your mind to these new thoughts increases neurotransmitters, and the emotional connection engages your brain's limbic system.

Following each scenario is a list of questions to help you explore your thoughts and emotions and rethink your fear. The questions stimulate both cognitive functioning and emotional intelligence. Repetition in the questions helps you establish healthy "go to bridges." Be sure to delve into these questions at your own pace, taking action over a period of time as you work toward resolving your fear. You may want to have a notebook or journal handy for making notes that you can review later.

Reminders to take a break and breathe have been incorporated to encourage you to rethink fear at a comfortable pace. Exploring fear can be stressful and you don't want to overwhelm yourself.

Those of you with deep-seated fears may require professional help. Counseling can provide new insights and be of great comfort. Many companies who provide healthcare for their employees also provide free Employee Assistance Programs (EAP). Check your employer for eligibility. If you do not have access to counseling through insurance, qualified counselors are available in most communities. Many of them provide services on a sliding fee scale to help make it affordable.

Rethinking fear can require a little or a lot of effort. It depends on what you want to change, how resistant you are to change and how clearly you understand you cannot change anyone else. Your fear is all about you and you alone.

As you go through the process of rethinking fear, consider the following truths:

- **Your brain is your power supply**. Be grateful for *and use* the abundance of neurotransmitters easily accessible to you. Open your mind to new ideas to increase neuron activity and create new "go to bridges."
- **You are accountable for your life choices.** You make the daily choices that affect your life. If you are not happy with them, don't blame others. Start making smarter choices.
- **Your happiness is solely your responsibility**. No one else can make you happy. Interaction with others can bring you joy, but happiness comes from within. By looking outward, you shirk your responsibility and unfairly burden others. This is your life, not theirs.
- **Your integrity shouts your worth**. Your worth is about who you are as a person. Be someone others can trust and admire. Hold your head high with honor. When you look into the mirror, let authenticity reflect back.
- **Your momentum in life is dependent upon your response to change**. The world is in fast-paced movement. The less resistant you are to change, the greater your ability to adapt, the easier you'll flow forward and succeed in life.
- **You have the right to ask for help without shame**. False pride holds no value. If your current group of family and friends is not supportive, look for assistance elsewhere. You are deserving of help.

- **You *are* worth the effort**. Your life has value. Creating fulfillment takes effort. You can hold yourself back with fear or move yourself forward with action. Taking action is the key to success. Stand brave and make the effort.

The way you live your life is your creation. It's constructed from your every thought, emotion and action. Consider those powerful neurotransmitters multiplying in your brain and take a moment to ask yourself, "What kind of bridges am I building today?"

THE VALUE OF
EMOTIONAL INTELLIGENCE

Emotional Intelligence (EI) has been woven into all of my training because success in life depends on your ability to communicate.

EI is all about people smarts. The better you understand your own and others emotions, the more you will trust yourself, the less fear you will experience and the more successful you will be at negotiation.

EI helps you move your locus of control from outside yourself to within. And making that shift helps you feel more capable and less fearful.

EI helps you stop blaming others for your lot in life and encourages you to step up and take accountability for your attitude, behavior and choices.

EI is about successfully understanding and using emotion.

EI is of great value because it allows you to:
- recognize your emotions which improves your reasoning and problem solving skills
- recognize others' emotions which helps you show empathy
- understand the difference in emotions which enhances your judgment
- express your emotions which helps you relate with others

The more specific your insight into your emotions, the better you can understand what caused the feeling and how to deal with it. For example, if you say you feel angry, what are you really feeling? Are you feeling annoyed, frustrated, anxious, hurt, defeated, fearful?

I recommend using the easy and helpful four W's (Who, When, Why, What) exercise to help better define emotion. Let's use the example of anger to walk through it.

Who am I angry with?
- The person I am with
- Someone else
- Myself

When did my anger start?
- This moment
- In the past
- Constantly recurring

Why do I feel angry?
- Reaction to something just said or done
- Old anger triggered by current event
- Don't have a clue

What do I want to do with my anger?
- Confront the person I'm angry with
- Process it alone or with a friend or therapist
- Process completed, can let it go

Think about using this exercise to better identify and understand your emotions whenever you find yourself feeling stressed or emotional. Repetition of the exercise can increase neurotransmitter function and create powerful EI "go to bridges" to help you maintain emotional balance.

The higher your Emotional Intelligence level, the more skills you possess for dealing with life's stresses. Below is a quiz in key EI categories for success in life. I often use quizzes like this in management training. It helps individuals self-assess and set self-improvement goals. Take a moment to rate yourself on a scale of 1 (low) to 5 (high). Take note of where you rated low in order to improve in those area.

Embracing Change	1	2	3	4	5
I adapt to new situations easily					
I embrace change in a positive manner					
I think others view me as flexible					

If you scored a 4 or 5, congratulate yourself on proactively embracing change. If you scored a 3, you have some flexibility, but could benefit from being a little more open to new experiences. If you scored a 2 or 1, you could improve your life by addressing your fear of change. Fearing change and viewing it as negative can threaten your success and happiness. By accepting upcoming changes, you can form a plan of action and feel more in control of the situation.

Understanding Strengths & Weaknesses	1	2	3	4	5
I understand what environments help me succeed					
I understand what pushes my buttons					
I think others view me as effective in handling my emotions					

If you scored a 4 or 5, congratulate yourself on having a clear understanding of your strengths and weaknesses. If you scored a 3, you have some insight, but could benefit from a little more observation. If you scored a 2 or 1, you could improve your life by addressing your fear of introspection. Having a clear awareness of both your good and bad behavior, improves your confidence. The goal is to know and use your talents to move you forward while learning to manage those emotions that hold you back.

Observing Others	1	2	3	4	5
I am curious about people					
I enjoy learning about our differences and similarities					
I think others view me as showing a high level of empathy					

If you scored a 4 or 5, congratulate yourself on having a high level of interpersonal comfort. If you scored a 3, you have some interest in others, but could benefit from extending yourself a little more. If you scored a 2 or 1, you could improve your life by addressing your lack of interest in others. Being curious about what makes people tick leads to empathy. Empathy leads to caring. The more you care about others and what they are going through, the better your interpersonal skills and the more genuine your relationships.

Judging Character	1	2	3	4	5
I can read people's hidden motives to know if I can trust them					
I have an understanding of what people are going through					
I think others view me as being skilled in social awareness					

If you scored a 4 or 5, congratulate yourself on your insight and ability to trust yourself. If you scored a 3, you have some level of trust, but could benefit from a little more practice in discernment. If you scored a 2 or 1, you could improve your life by addressing your lack of trust. The ability to read other people and notice what is hidden beneath the surface is important in knowing whether or not you can trust them. Judging character is not about your trust in others; it is about your trust in yourself. When you trust your ability to understand what motivates others, you feel safer.

Developing Self-Confidence	1	2	3	4	5
I know who I am and don't allow what people say to bother me					
I don't waste time and energy holding grudges					
I think others view me as confident, open minded and joyful					

If you scored a 4 or 5, congratulate yourself on your high level of confidence and freedom. If you scored a 3, you have some confidence, but could benefit from not allowing others to stress you. If you scored a 2 or 1, you could improve your life by addressing your lack of confidence. Expressing yourself as open-minded and joyful shows others you have confidence and will not allow what they say or do to bother you. Holding grudges is a waste of time. Holding grudges gives others power over your life. While you keep re-stressing yourself over what they did, they are off enjoying life. Letting go of grudges and learning to roll with life's punches gives you freedom.

Abandoning Perfection	1	2	3	4	5
I know everyone makes mistakes and try to learn from mine					
I never beat myself up if I make a mistake					
I think others view me as turning failures into learning lessons					

If you scored a 4 or 5, congratulate yourself on your having the ability to learn and let go. If you scored a 3, you have reasonable expectations, but could benefit from giving yourself more breaks. If you scored a 2 or 1, you could improve your life by addressing your fear of failure. None of us is perfect. Your expectations of yourself need to be reasonable rather than unrealistic. Accepting that you are not perfect while striving to improve your skills can help you reach a balance between beating yourself up and dismissing mistakes completely.

Saying No	1	2	3	4	5
I honor my current commitments before taking on new projects					
I have no problem saying "No" to control my stress levels					
I think others view me as honest and helpful					

If you scored a 4 or 5, congratulate yourself on your ability to negotiate your needs. If you scored a 3, you know how to decline, but could benefit from putting yourself first more often. If you scored a 2 or 1, you could improve your life by addressing your fear of saying "No." You can avoid stress and burnout by honoring and successfully fulfilling your existing commitments before taking on new projects. Pushing yourself to the breaking point is unhealthy and keeps you from doing your best. Saying "No" shows respect for yourself and others.

Avoiding Toxic People	1	2	3	4	5
I make a point to limit my interactions with toxic people					
I don't let toxic people suck me into their chaos					
I think others view me as rational and reasonable					

If you scored a 4 or 5, congratulate yourself on your ability to side-step unreasonable people. If you scored a 3, you have protective instincts, but could benefit from not allowing others to suck you in. If you scored a 2 or 1, you could improve your life by addressing your lack of self-protection. Toxic people enjoy confrontation and chaos. They can be emotionally exhausting. The best way to take care of yourself is to limit your interactions with them. If you must interact, remain calm and communicate from a rational and reasonable position.

Being Grateful	1	2	3	4	5
I make time every day to be grateful for all I have					
I don't fret about what I don't have					
I think others view me as being appreciative					

If you scored a 4 or 5, congratulate yourself on thoroughly appreciating what you have accomplished. If you scored a 3, you have some appreciation, but could benefit from taking a little more time to assess your successes. If you scored a 2 or 1, you could improve your life by taking the time to address your achievements. Daily expression of gratitude for your family, friends and achievements refocuses you on what's real in your life. Fretting about what you lack is a waste of time and only serves to defeat you. Contemplating gratitude for the good in your life lifts your mood and energy levels, increases your optimism and opens you to new opportunities.

So, what did this exercise help you to learn about yourself? Are you better able to recognize and value your EI strengths? Are there areas where you feel you need improvement?

By strengthening your Emotional Intelligence, you increase your confidence in your ability to handle life's stresses and fears.

Improving your life is an on-going learning process. You *are* worth the effort.

A

ALEX THE ANXIOUS ALLIGATOR

Alex was a strikingly handsome alligator. Not only were his proportions perfectly precise, his tail held a tinge of chartreuse, making him quite an impressive specimen.

As luck would have it, Alex's boss, Owen, held no appreciation for individuality. Owen valued conformity.

All of the alligators in the office were furnished grey metal desks. They all had to use only company-inscribed black ink pens. And, most importantly, all had to sign their paperwork with their right hands.

Alex's colorful tail was tolerated due to his high repeat sales. For the one thing Owen valued more than conformity was repeat business.

Alex did his best to blend in, because he had something more than the color of his tail to get him fired. Alex held a deep secret. He was born left-handed. He had learned to use his right hand in his work, but he kept guard over his left so as not to allow it to perform naturally.

Only when away from work did Alex feel free to allow left-handed expression. He twirled intricate designs, configured complex patterns and created beautiful works of art. None of which he was capable of doing with his right hand. He had developed a clearly divided system of living…freedom left; work right.

One day when business was slow, Alex designed a rather impressive new company logo. Studying it pleasingly, he suddenly realized he was using his left hand. He looked around quickly and sighed with relief that no one seemed to have noticed. Unable to bring himself to tear up the creative design, he folded it and hid it in his desk drawer.

The next day, Owen called Alex into his office. "I found this in your desk," said Owen, holding up the creative logo. Owen made a habit of going through his employees' desks. "Did you do it?"

"Yes, sir," admitted Alex recognizing the design. He was certain he'd be fired.

"It's good. I'm going to use it as our new logo. The printer will need an unfolded one. Draw it again," said Owen, pushing a pad and pen across the desk to Alex.

Fear flooded over Alex. If he used his left hand, he would be fired for violating the right hand rule. If he used his right, he would be fired for being unable to recreate the design. What to do?

Figuring he'd be fired either way, Alex decided to tell the truth. He looked directly into his boss's eyes and stated, "Sir, I work with my right hand, but I can draw only with my left."

Owen stared back at him without comment. After a few moments, he picked up a pen with his left hand and with awkward strokes signed his name on the pad in front of him. "It's been forty years since I've written with this hand. They made me switch in grade school. Told me I'd never amount to anything if I didn't use my right hand. You can use whatever hand you want to recreate that logo."

If our natural abilities defy the norm, do we allow fear to divide our talents or do we practice an ambidextrous system of living?

Rethinking Fear Exercise A
Fear of Failure, Fear of Disclosing a Secret

It seems both Owen and Alex were afraid to allow themselves to *be* themselves. Owen allowed a childhood falsehood to create a lifelong fear of failure and he perpetuated his fear onto his employees. Alex allowed his fear of looking different and his fear of Owen's standards to smother his valuable artistic talents. Let's examine the fears of Owen and Alex separately.

OWEN

Maybe, like Owen, you were told something in childhood that triggers fear for you and affects your decisions to this day? Maybe, like Owen, you have never stopped to think if what you were told is true?

What if you took a moment *right now* to begin to rethink that fearful message and observe how you have allowed it to affect your thinking and behavior? You can start by asking yourself the following questions.

Thoughts:
What is the message I have been telling myself?
Who was the person who first told it to me?
What was happening when it was said?
Was anyone else in the room?
What was their response?
What was my response?
If I had none at the time, do I have one now? What is it?
Do I believe the message I was told is true?
If I do not believe it is true, what true message will I use to replace the untrue message?
Your brain has power. What ideas come to mind on how you can resolve this fear? List them.

Emotions:
What did I feel while it was being said?
What did I feel after it was said?
What am I feeling today?
Do I want to practice the four W's (Who, When, Why, What) from the Value of Emotional Intelligence Chapter to help better define my emotions about my fear of failure?
Your emotional and physical health are important. Are you suffering from depression or anxiety and need to speak with your doctor? Do you feel you could benefit from counseling? If so, what steps do you need to take to seek help through services available to you? Take action now.

Life Impact:
How is my fear of failure affecting:
My relationships?
My health?
My work?
My happiness?
Your life is your creation. Your thoughts, emotions and actions create reactions. What impact has your fear of failure had on your life so far? Are you willing to make changes?

Moving Forward:
What kind of healthy neurotransmitter bridges did I build today?
Your new thoughts and emotions about your fear of failure increased your neurotransmitters and created new "go to bridges" for you to use in the future. Continue improving your life.
Congratulate yourself for taking the action to rethink your fear! You are worth the effort!

Take a Break and Breathe:
Rethinking fear can be stressful, so don't overwhelm yourself.
Raise your hands in the air and stretch.
Take a deep breath.
Smile.
Take the dog for a walk.
Pet the cat.
Call a friend.
Eat a piece of chocolate.
Do something that relaxes you.
Step away from the book.

ALEX

Maybe, like Alex, you look a little different from your friends and have allowed your fear of not blending in to minimize or ridicule your difference? Maybe, like Alex, you hold a secret that you are afraid your friends or employer might discover? Maybe your fear causes you to lead two lives?

What if you took a moment *right now* to begin to rethink your fear of disclosing that secret and examine how you have allowed it to affect your thinking and behavior? You can start by asking yourself the following questions.

Thoughts:
What is the secret I am hiding from others?
Why do I feel I need to keep this secret?
Do I know anyone else who has a secret similar to mine?
What happened to them because of disclosing?
Is it logical that I will incur a similar consequence?
Have I thought about disclosing my secret to a trusted friend?
Do I have a plan about how to do that?
Your brain has power. What ideas come to mind on how you can resolve this fear? List them.

Emotions:
What is my fear associated with disclosing my secret?
Is my fear imagined or are there actual consequences to disclosing my secret?
What are the consequences? List them.
What is my fear of disclosing to a trusted friend?
Do I have a plan to protect myself if my fear is proven true?
Do I want to practice the four W's (Who, When, Why, What) from the Value of Emotional Intelligence chapter to help better define my emotions about my fear of disclosing?
Your emotional and physical health are important. Are you suffering from depression or anxiety and need to speak with your doctor? Do you feel you could benefit from counseling? What steps do you need to take to seek help through services available to you? Take action now.

| **Life Impact:** |
| How is my fear of disclosing my secret affecting: |
| My relationships? |
| My health? |
| My work? |
| My happiness? |
| Your life is your creation. Your thoughts, emotions and actions create reactions. What impact has your fear of disclosing your secret had on your life so far? Are you willing to make changes? |

| **Moving Forward:** |
| What kind of healthy neurotransmitter bridges did I build today? |
| Your new thoughts and emotions about your fear of disclosing your secret increased your neurotransmitters and created new "go to bridges" for you to use in the future. Continue improving your life. |
| **Congratulate yourself for taking the action to rethink your fear! You are worth the effort!** |

| **Take a Break and Breathe:** |
| Rethinking fear can be stressful, so don't overwhelm yourself. |
| Raise your hands in the air and stretch. |
| Take a deep breath. |
| Smile. |
| Take the dog for a walk. |
| Pet the cat. |
| Call a friend. |
| Eat a piece of chocolate. |
| Do something that relaxes you. |
| Step away from the book. |

B

THE BADGER AND THE BUTTERFLY

Many years ago, a badger family named Smythe lived in a complex series of chambers with multiple tunnels leading up to the forest floor. Scottie Smythe, the youngest son, loved to explore the often unused tunnels to sneak out at night to snack.

One night, as he was enjoying some elder-berries, he noticed a butterfly sleeping inside the bush. He had often eaten earthworms, but hadn't tried a butterfly. Just as he was reaching in to grab it, it awakened and flew away.

Its expanded wings displayed its beautifully colored pattern. Having never seen a butterfly up close, Scottie was struck by its splendor and chased after it for some distance. It finally rested in a tree high above him.

Scottie had barely begun scooting up the trunk when the butterfly took off and the chase was on again. Scottie pursued the butterfly with total focus. Soon, he found himself all alone in the deepest part of the forest. No butterfly. No badger family. No idea how to get home.

At first he felt afraid, but then he noticed some bluebell bulbs, realized he was hungry and began nibbling on them. After having his fill, Scottie curled up in the nearby brush and settled in for the night.

Morning came and Scottie found some plump grubs for breakfast. He discovered lots of new things to do in this part of the forest. He chased a rabbit and a hedgehog and ran up and down the fallen tree trunks. After a fun day of play, Scottie wanted to go home, but he had chased the butterfly far from recognizable surroundings.

Which way was home? North? South? East? West? If he chose the wrong direction, he'd move even farther away from home. Feeling afraid and alone, Scottie sat on the ground and wept, going nowhere.

Just as the sun was setting, Scottie felt a flapping above his head. He looked up and there was the butterfly he had chased into the forest.

"Are you lost?" asked the butterfly.

"Yes!" answered Scottie. "I want to go home."

"I'll take you home if you promise not to eat me," offered the butterfly.

"I promise," vowed Scottie, anxious to get home.

Both remained true to their words. Scottie got back home safely and the butterfly wasn't eaten.

When lost in the decision making process, are we left to struggle alone or are we willing to reach a compromise with an unlikely friend?

Rethinking Fear Exercise B
Fear of Trusting

Both the badger and the butterfly had to make a decision whether to trust one another. Scottie had to trust the butterfly to get him home. The butterfly had to trust Scottie not to eat him. Trust requires taking a risk.

Maybe, like the badger and the butterfly, you want to trust someone but fear getting hurt? Maybe someone shattered your trust in the past and so you are afraid to trust again?

What if you took a moment *right now* to begin to rethink your fear of trusting and observe how you have allowed it to affect your thinking and behavior? You can start by asking yourself the following questions.

Thoughts:
What was the incident that shattered my trust?
Did I tell the person who hurt me how I felt?
What was their response to me?
What was my response?
Is there someone in my life now I would like to trust?
Why do I want to reach out to this person?
Do I believe trust is an all or nothing situation?
Am I willing to begin with levels of trust, building upon each layer?
Am I someone others can trust?
If not, does my fear have to do with someone doing to me what I have done to others?
If so, am I willing to change my thinking and behavior and become someone trustworthy?
Your brain has power. What ideas come to mind on how you can resolve this fear? List them.

Emotions:
Have I processed my pain over my previous trust issue?
Am I looking for revenge or am I sincere about resolving the trust issue?
What do I need to do to resolve those feelings and move on?
Is this a healthy approach or am I setting myself up for more pain?
Am I ready to let this go or am I holding false hope of reconciliation?
Does my gut tell me this new person seems trustworthy?
What am I afraid might happen if I trust this person?
What is the likelihood that will happen? 10%? 90%?
If the worst happens, do I have a plan in mind to deal with my hurt?
Do I want to practice the four W's (Who, When, Why, What) from the Value of Emotional Intelligence Chapter to help better define my emotions about my fear of trusting?
Your emotional and physical health are important. Are you suffering from depression or anxiety and need to speak with your doctor? Do you feel you could benefit from counseling? What steps do you need to take to seek help through services available to you? Take action now.

Life Impact:
How is my fear of trusting affecting:
My relationships?
My health?
My work?
My happiness?
Your life is your creation. Your thoughts, emotions and actions create reactions. What impact has your fear of trusting had on your life so far? Are you willing to make changes?

Moving Forward:
What kind of healthy neurotransmitter bridges did I build today?
Your new thoughts and emotions about your fear of trusting increased your neurotransmitters and created new "go to bridges" for you to use in the future. Continue improving your life.
Congratulate yourself for taking the action to rethink your fear! You are worth the effort!

Take a Break and Breathe:
Rethinking fear can be stressful, so don't overwhelm yourself.
Raise your hands in the air and stretch.
Take a deep breath.
Smile.
Take the dog for a walk.
Pet the cat.
Call a friend.
Eat a piece of chocolate.
Do something that relaxes you.
Step away from the book.

CASEY THE CANTANKEROUS CAMEL

Casey trudged across the desert with resentment. He cursed at the burning sun and kicked with frustration at smaller desert creatures. He believed the desert his enemy and his daily journey a burden he must bear.

"You can't defeat me, desert. I'll fight you and survive," spat Casey in a fit of fury. Casey often ranted about the discomforts he viewed as his life's curse.

One day, as Casey's sand-encrusted calves marched angrily, yet steadily, along, he happened across an abnormally large and brilliant turquoise scorpion. Struck by its size, Casey kicked it aside rather than squishing it dead.

"Hey! Who are you to kick me?" yelled the scorpion crawling quickly up Casey's leg.

"You were in my way," Casey yelled back.

"I most certainly was not," stated the scorpion firmly.

"Okay, okay. Maybe not," conceded Casey. "Now, move along. I'm in a hurry."

"You have a very unpleasant manner."

"Look, I've got a heavy burden, a pressing deadline, and you're holding me up. Beat it."

"Why do you have to be so nasty? You'd have a much easier trip if you'd make friends. Why not ask the desert for help?" suggested the scorpion.

"Ask it for help? Just how can this sadistic desert help me?" asked Casey sarcastically.

"Oh, the desert is full of wondrous treasures," informed the scorpion. "It treats me very kindly and brings me much joy."

"Well, your wonderful desert has provided me with nothing so far and I don't see any way this cursed place will improve. So, get out of my way. I'm in a hurry," ordered Casey. And flinging the scorpion ten feet with the flick of his ankle, he continued on his journey.

"You might find the desert a lot more enjoyable if you improved your disposition!" called the scorpion after him.

If our life experiences are constantly unpleasant, is it a curse of fate or a reflection of our attitude?

Rethinking Fear Exercise C
Fear of Being Stuck

Casey focused on the negatives of his experience and made his travels through the desert much more disagreeable than they needed to be.

Maybe, like Casey, you find yourself in a situation that is unpleasant for you? Maybe you don't see a way out and fear you'll be stuck forever enduring what you hate? Maybe you complain about it? Maybe you take your anger out on others? Maybe you feel jealousy and resentment toward others you deem have an easier life?

What if you took a moment *right now* to rethink your fear of being stuck in a situation you don't want to be in and observe how you have allowed this to affect your thinking and behavior? You can start by asking yourself the following questions.

Thoughts:
If I don't want what I have, do I know what I want?
Do I understand that only I, not things or others, can make me happy?
Do I understand I have the power to change my situation by changing my actions?
If I don't understand this, what can help me better understand cause and effect?
Am I willing to assess the positives in my life and focus on gratitude?
Am I willing to stop complaining about my situation?
Am I willing to take positive action to improve my situation?
Am I willing to take classes or educate myself in an effort to move forward in life?
Your brain has power. What ideas come to mind on how you can resolve this fear? List them.

Emotions:
What emotional fulfillment do I get from complaining?
What is the thing I fear most about feeling stuck in this situation?
What is the probability of that happening?
If the worst happens, do I have a plan in mind to address it so that I won't feel so afraid?
Am I feeling my life is out of my control?
What one thing can I do today that will help me feel less stuck?
Do I want to practice the four W's (Who, When, Why, What) from the Value of Emotional Intelligence Chapter to help better define my emotions about my fear of being stuck?
Your emotional and physical health are important. Are you suffering from depression or anxiety and need to speak with your doctor? Do you feel you could benefit from counseling? What steps do you need to take to seek help through services available to you? Take action now.

Life Impact:
How is my fear of being stuck affecting:
My relationships?
My health?
My work?
My happiness?
Your life is your creation. Your thoughts, emotions and actions create reactions. What impact has your fear of being stuck had on your life so far? Are you willing to make changes?

Moving Forward:
What kind of healthy neurotransmitter bridges did I build today?
Your new thoughts and emotions about your fear of being stuck increased your neurotransmitters and created new "go to bridges" for you to use in the future. Continue improving your life.
Congratulate yourself for taking the action to rethink your fear! You are worth the effort!

Take a Break and Breathe:
Rethinking fear can be stressful, so don't overwhelm yourself.
Raise your hands in the air and stretch.
Take a deep breath.
Smile.
Take the dog for a walk.
Pet the cat.
Call a friend.
Eat a piece of chocolate.
Do something that relaxes you.
Step away from the book.

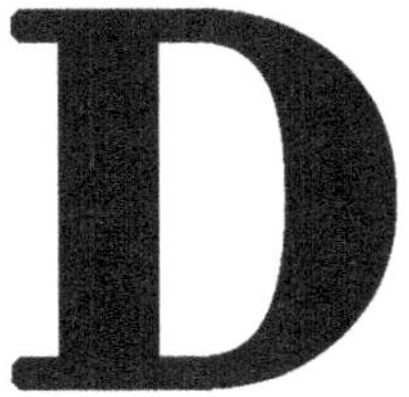

DONALD THE DEFENSIVE DONKEY

Donald, regarded as a docile donkey, was given the assignment of guarding the valuable race horses in the north stable. His task was to be a calming influence over the high-strung assets.

Taking his responsibilities seriously, Donald monitored the horses closely night and day. This continuous monitoring soon became exhausting…for both him and the horses.

As Donald became more fatigued, he became more fearful something would happen to the horses. He didn't share his concerns with them. He increased his scrutiny.

Because Donald didn't communicate with the horses, the horses didn't communicate with Donald. They didn't tell him that sensing his fear and his constant surveillance made them uneasy.

Both Donald and the horses felt stressed and unhappy.

One day, Roger, the donkey from the west stable, ambled by. "Need some help?"

"It's under control," brayed Donald defensively.

"Can't fool me," Roger said knowingly. "I recognize the sweat of fear on your back."

"Look. I know how to protect these horses," assured Donald.

"Like a jailer," stated Roger.

"What does that mean?" asked Donald.

"It means you try to control them instead of communicating with them. Why don't you try getting to know them?"

"I wasn't hired to be their friend," defended Donald.

"They can sense your fear, you know," advised Roger.

Donald knew if the horses sensed his fear, they would not remain calm and could hurt themselves. He had allowed his fear to put them in danger. Donald's ears drooped and he lowered his head in shame. "What do I need to do?"

Roger smiled kindly at Donald. "Try changing your focus. Don't think so much about the bad that might happen and enjoy your time with the horses. Relax a little. Get to know them. Let them know what you are doing and why. Be their friend."

"The horses are uncomfortable with me right now. Do you think they'd forgive the way I've acted and be willing to be my friends?" asked Donald.

"Be honest and kind to them and they'll friend you," advised Roger.

If changing our focus can help our relationship, do we continue to focus inward with fear or venture outward with optimism?

Rethinking Fear Exercise D
Fear of Something Going Wrong

If Donald had communicated with the horses from the start, he would have established a sense of trust and the horses would have been more comfortable. Donald could have been less controlling and all would have been less stressed.

Maybe, like Donald, you find yourself in a situation where you feel responsible for something or someone and are worried it will go wrong if you aren't vigilant? Maybe your vigilance comes across as controlling which makes others uncomfortable and want to pull away from you? Maybe you are feeling stressed and alone and afraid?

What if you took a moment *right now* to begin to rethink your fear of something going wrong and observe how you have allowed this to affect your thinking and behavior? You can start by asking yourself the following questions.

Thoughts:
What is the worst that could happen if I let my guard down?
Is that probable, possible or an excuse to control?
Do I have a plan to handle what might happen?
Is my vigilance and worry about protecting others or is it about my having control?
Am I willing to accept that control is about me and not others?
Am I willing to change my behavior to establish a better relationship with others?
Your brain has power. What ideas come to mind on how you can resolve this fear? List them.

Emotions:
When am I most fearful about something going wrong? Is it at certain times, in certain places or with certain people?
What is it about those times, places or people that trigger me?
When I am not in control, how do I respond?
What emotional fulfillment do I get from trying to control events or others?
What is the underlying fear I am using my control to hide?
Do I want to practice the four W's (Who, When, Why, What) from the Value of Emotional Intelligence Chapter to help better define my emotions about my fear of something going wrong?
Your emotional and physical health are important. Are you suffering from depression or anxiety and need to speak with your doctor? Do you feel you could benefit from counseling? What steps do you need to take to seek help through services available to you? Take action now.

Life Impact:
How is my fear of something going wrong affecting:
My relationships?
My health?
My work?
My happiness?
Your life is your creation. Your thoughts, emotions and actions create reactions. What impact has your fear of something going wrong had on your life so far? Are you willing to make changes?

Moving Forward:
What kind of healthy neurotransmitter bridges did I build today?
Your new thoughts and emotions about your fear of something going wrong increased your neurotransmitters and created new "go to bridges" for you to use in the future.   Continue improving your life.
Congratulate yourself for taking the action to rethink your fear! You are worth the effort!

Take a Break and Breathe:
Rethinking fear can be stressful, so don't overwhelm yourself.
Raise your hands in the air and stretch.
Take a deep breath.
Smile.
Take the dog for a walk.
Pet the cat.
Call a friend.
Eat a piece of chocolate.
Do something that relaxes you.
Step away from the book.

E

THE EKING EWES

In a small village far from town lived three very poor ewes...Dolly, Molly, and Polly. Each day, they traveled the rough road into the city to earn feed for their families.

Not only was traversing the stony road difficult, but the city was polluted and the work was physically and emotionally draining. Often, one or another of the village ewes took ill. The others would help support her until she was well again. Somehow, they all managed to eke by, but life was hard.

One day, all three village ewes were too sick to travel.

Dolly said, "Oh no! Who will go to the city to toil?"

Molly said, "I'm the sickest."

Polly said, "With so little left in the pen, how will we feed our kids?"

With all their struggles, none needed this added burden.

Dolly faced her sickness with fear. She felt victimized and cursed the sickness. She thought it unfair that this had happened to her rather than to some rich farmer's ewe with means. Wasn't her life already burdened? Why was she being punished this way? She focused upon her sickness and worried about her future. If she became sicker or died, who would support her family? She gulped down her medicine and cried. Her heart was heavy with bitterness. She defeated herself with self-pity.

Molly faced her sickness with bravado. She puffed out her chest and bragged about her sickness. She ignored her need for rest and walked proudly throughout the village asking for work. She found pleasure in the attention the sickness provided. She denied her body care and infected others in the village with her sickness. Her heart was filled with pride. Her reward was superficial, for she hurt herself and others with her selfishness.

Polly faced her sickness with resolve. She took her medicine and rested to help herself heal more quickly. She used her physical confinement to reflect on her life. She assessed her strengths and her weaknesses. She noted steps she could take to make changes in herself and her life. She discovered a plan to feed her kids without having to go to the city. When self-pity and doubt filled her mind, she tried to understand her feelings and used them for growth. She learned much about herself and soon grew strong. The changes she had made allowed her to take the steps to a better life.

If the trials of life are opportunities for growth, does our attitude become our reality?

Rethinking Fear Exercise E
Fear of Carrying a Burden

The ewes reacted differently to the same situation. Dolly chose anger and self-pity. Molly sought attention through bravado. Polly cared for herself and used the time to consider a plan of action.

Maybe, like the ewes, you find yourself in a situation where you feel burdened? Maybe you are dealing with family, financial or health issues? Maybe you are feeling worried, depleted and afraid?

Maybe, like Dolly, you are feeling angry that life isn't fair? Maybe you complain too often to others? Maybe to make yourself feel better you demean others you think have lesser problems?

Maybe, like Molly, you feel the need for attention? Maybe you put on a brave face so others will applaud your strength? Maybe you cling to the applause to get yourself through? Maybe you are hiding the tears behind the brave mask, but feel you must continue the game?

What if you took a moment *right now* to begin to rethink your fear of carrying a burden and observe how you have allowed this to affect your thinking and behavior? You can start by asking yourself the following questions.

Thoughts:
Is this a burden I must carry alone?
Am I willing to ask someone else to help me?
Am I willing to take positive action and stop complaining about my burden?
Do I understand I have the power to change my situation by changing my attitude?
Your brain has power. What ideas come to mind on how you can resolve this fear? List them.

Emotions:
Do I feel anger about carrying this burden?
Do I resent someone who is not helping?
Did I ask the person to help and they refused or did I expect them to read my mind that I need help?
What emotional fulfillment do I get from complaining or acting brave about this burden?
What is the underlying fear my burden represents?
Do I want to practice the four W's (Who, When, Why, What) from the Value of Emotional Intelligence Chapter to help better define my emotions about my fear of carrying a burden?
Your emotional and physical health are important. Are you suffering from depression or anxiety and need to speak with your doctor? Do you feel you could benefit from counseling? What steps do you need to take to seek help through services available to you? Take action now.

Life Impact:
How is my fear of carrying a burden affecting:
My relationships?
My health?
My work?
My happiness?
Your life is your creation. Your thoughts, emotions and actions create reactions. What impact has your fear of carrying a burden had on your life so far? Are you willing to make changes?

Moving Forward:
What kind of healthy neurotransmitter bridges did I build today?
Your new thoughts and emotions about your fear of carrying a burden increased your neurotransmitters and created new "go to bridges" for you to use in the future.   Continue improving your life.
Congratulate yourself for taking the action to rethink your fear! You are worth the effort!

Take a Break and Breathe:
Rethinking fear can be stressful, so don't overwhelm yourself.
Raise your hands in the air and stretch.
Take a deep breath.
Smile.
Take the dog for a walk.
Pet the cat.
Call a friend.
Eat a piece of chocolate.
Do something that relaxes you.
Step away from the book.

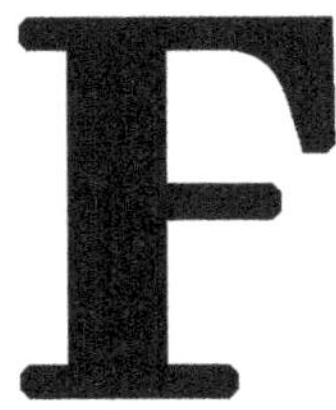

FLORENCE THE FUSSY FELINE

Florence was as pretty as she was persnickety. She had clear bright eyes, a soft grey coat that gleamed from healthy food and loving attention, and a very self-serving attitude.

Although her owner provided her with everything she could possibly need, Florence was rarely appreciative and seldom satisfied.

There were even times when Florence deemed gifts inferior and insisted they be given to Charity (the cat next door) and then demanded something bigger or better.

One day, Florence was presented with a beautifully wrapped package. Talented at correctly guessing a gift from the size and shape of its box, Florence concluded that this box was too wide and certainly not long enough for what she really wanted…a new scratching post.

Offering her owner an expression of disdain, Florence sighed pettishly and batted the package aside. "Since this obviously isn't my new scratching post, I won't bother to open it."

"Are you sure you don't want to open it, Florence?" coaxed her owner.

"I'm sure," hissed Florence fussily. "Take it away and give it to Charity."

"As you wish," answered her owner, who took the package away and gave it to Charity.

The next day, as Florence lay on the window-sill soaking up the noon sun, she noticed Charity happily climbing up and down the tallest scratching post Florence had ever seen.

Pouncing over to her owner, Florence howled, "If you loved me, you would have gotten me that." She pointed enviously at Charity's scratching post.

"But I did, Florence," assured her owner. "That was the present you wouldn't open."

"Impossible. That box wasn't long enough for something that tall," protested Florence.

"It was packaged unassembled," informed her owner.

Shocked, Florence sat back on her haunches and meowed sadly.

If we think life's not giving us what we ask for, maybe it just needs to be assembled.

Rethinking Fear Exercise F
Fear of Not Being the Focus

Florence lost out because she acted spoiled, demanding and unappreciative.

Maybe, like Florence, you find it hard to appreciate what others do for you? Maybe you don't appear grateful for what has been given to you? Maybe you enjoy being the focus of attention and don't extend yourself to others? Maybe your behavior has caused others to distance from you? Maybe this distance has caused you to feel isolated? Maybe your feelings frighten you and cause you to be more demanding?

What if you took a moment *right now* to begin to rethink your fear of not being the focus and observe how you have allowed this to affect your thinking and behavior? You can start by asking yourself the following questions.

Thoughts:
Do I understand I have value whether I am the focus, on the side or out of the room?
Do I realize my demanding behavior is disrespectful to others?
Do I understand I have the power to change my behavior anytime I want?
Am I willing to examine my behavior and improve?
Am I willing to be grateful for what others do for me?
Am I willing to rebuild relationships based on mutual respect?
Your brain has power. What ideas come to mind on how you can resolve this fear? List them.

Emotions:
Am I outwardly acting better than others because inwardly I feel less than others?
Am I afraid that acting appreciative makes me vulnerable?
Is being demanding how I express anger?
Can I see how this is an unhealthy expression of anger?
What emotional fulfillment do I get from being the focus of attention?
What do I feel a lack of that causes me to be demanding of others?
Do I want to practice the four W's (Who, When, Why, What) from the Value of Emotional Intelligence Chapter to help better define my emotions about my fear of not being the focus?
Your emotional and physical health are important. Are you suffering from depression or anxiety and need to speak with your doctor? Do you feel you could benefit from counseling? What steps do you need to take to seek help through services available to you? Take action now.

Life Impact:
How is my fear of not being the focus affecting:
My relationships?
My health?
My work?
My happiness?
Your life is your creation. Your thoughts, emotions and actions create reactions. What impact has your fear of not being the focus had on your life so far? Are you willing to make changes?

Moving Forward:
What kind of healthy neurotransmitter bridges did I build today?
Your new thoughts and emotions about your fear of not being the focus increased your neurotransmitters and created new "go to bridges" for you to use in the future.   Continue improving your life.
Congratulate yourself for taking the action to rethink your fear! You are worth the effort!

Take a Break and Breathe:
Rethinking fear can be stressful, so don't overwhelm yourself.
Raise your hands in the air and stretch.
Take a deep breath.
Smile.
Take the dog for a walk.
Pet the cat.
Call a friend.
Eat a piece of chocolate.
Do something that relaxes you.
Step away from the book.

G

GILBERT THE GULLIBLE GUPPY

Once upon a time, in a crystal clear fish tank, lived a happy guppy named Gilbert.

Gilbert had everything a guppy could want…a clean tank lined with colorful pebbles, a miniature castle, little green plants, and, of course, the exact amount of food daily.

One day, another fish was dropped into Gilbert's tank. Happy to have a friend, Gilbert approached the new addition excitedly. "Hi! I'm Gilbert. Who are you?"

"They call me Speedy 'cause I swim fast." Speedy demonstrated by circling the tank in an instant. "See?" he said, flashing a conceited grin.

"Oh, yes. What fun. Will you teach me how to do that?" asked Gilbert.

"Sorry, kid, but it can't be taught. You either got it or you don't. It's a natural talent."

"Oh, I see. I guess that's best. If we both swam fast, we might run into one another," said Gilbert, laughing.

"Sure, kid," dismissed Speedy. "Say, it's kind of small here," he complained, surveying the tank critically. "Clean though," he conceded.

"Oh, it gets scrubbed every week," informed Gilbert. "It's an exciting adventure. I get scooped out with a little net and put in another tank until this one is cleaned."

"Sounds like a real trip," said Speedy sarcastically. "So, how long you been here, kid?"

"All my life. I was born here," said Gilbert proudly.

"Whoa! No wonder you thrill easy," gibed Speedy. "You know, kid, this here isn't real life. I know what I'm talking about. Where I come from, giant tanks are filled with hundreds of fish, all kinds, all in the same room. I seen some tropical beauties would knock your eyes out. Ah, the stories I could tell."

"Oh, please, tell me? It sounds very exciting."

"Sure, kid, later," deferred Speedy. "Now, about living arrangements. I'll need my privacy, so I'm taking over the castle. I figure you'd want me to be comfortable. Now, as for food, I'm what you call a heavy eater. So, we'll split it seventy/thirty. I figure you want me to keep up my strength so I can swim fast for you and feel up to telling you my exciting stories. And I want to do those favors for you."

"You do? Oh, this is going to be such fun. It's so nice having you here. I just know we're going to be great friends."

"Sure, kid. Looks like this place might be okay after all," assessed Speedy with a knowing smile.

Within a month, Speedy was totally bored. Even though he had complete control of the castle, ate seventy-five percent of the food and knocked Gilbert comically around with his frantic swimming, he felt unfulfilled.

Gilbert found he wasn't nearly as happy living with Speedy as he had been living alone. He missed his freedom. Occasionally, he cautioned Speedy about the dangers of overeating, hoping Speedy would leave him a little more food. Mostly, Gilbert remained quiet and tried to stay out of Speedy's way.

One morning, Gilbert awoke to find Speedy gone. After several days of waiting for him to return, Gilbert realized that Speedy wasn't coming back. He grinned broadly and swam in and out of the castle in celebration.

"Oh, freedom, wonderful freedom," he sang. "I'll never give you up again."

If we allow our freedom to be duped by others, is the fault theirs or ours?

Rethinking Fear Exercise G

Fear of Speaking Up

One might say that Gilbert was duped by Speedy. Certainly, Gilbert was naïve and initially taken in by Speedy's pizzazz. However, when Gilbert realized he was unhappy with the living arrangement, he chose not to speak up, even though he had the power to do so.

Maybe, like Gilbert, you are living in an unpleasant arrangement? Maybe you are allowing someone to take advantage of you? Maybe you are unhappy living a life you don't want to live? Maybe you are afraid to speak up?

What if you took a moment *right now* to begin to rethink your fear of speaking up and observe how you have allowed this to affect your thinking and behavior? You can start by asking yourself the following questions.

Thoughts:
Do I understand I have a responsibility to myself to speak up?
Am I willing to leave a bad relationship or job for my freedom?
Do I understand to seek help if I am in an abusive situation?
Am I willing to prepare an exit plan?
Will the time frame meet my needs?
Am I willing to build my confidence by practicing my speech with a friend?
Do I have a support system in place for after I speak up?
Your brain has power. What ideas come to mind on how you can resolve this fear? List them.

Emotions:
Do I feel undeserving of speaking up for myself?
Am I feeling unhappy in my current life situation?
What am I afraid will happen if I speak up?
What is the probability of that happening?
Do I have a plan to protect myself should that happen?
Do I want to practice the four W's (Who, When, Why, What) from the Value of Emotional Intelligence Chapter to help better define my emotions about my fear of speaking up?
Your emotional and physical health are important. Are you suffering from depression or anxiety and need to speak with your doctor? Do you feel you could benefit from counseling? What steps do you need to take to seek help through services available to you? Take action now.

Life Impact:
How is my fear of speaking up affecting:
My relationships?
My health?
My work?
My happiness?
Your life is your creation. Your thoughts, emotions and actions create reactions. What impact has your fear of speaking up had on your life so far? Are you willing to make changes?

Moving Forward:
What kind of healthy neurotransmitter bridges did I build today?
Your new thoughts and emotions about your fear of speaking up increased your neurotransmitters and created new "go to bridges" for you to use in the future. Continue improving your life.
Congratulate yourself for taking the action to rethink your fear! You are worth the effort!

Take a Break and Breathe:
Rethinking fear can be stressful, so don't overwhelm yourself.
Raise your hands in the air and stretch.
Take a deep breath.
Smile.
Take the dog for a walk.
Pet the cat.
Call a friend.
Eat a piece of chocolate.
Do something that relaxes you.
Step away from the book.

H

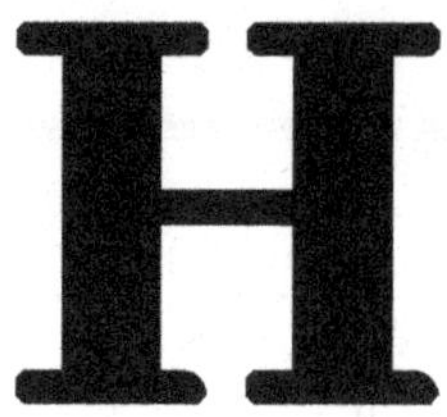

HARRY THE HARRIED HARDTOP

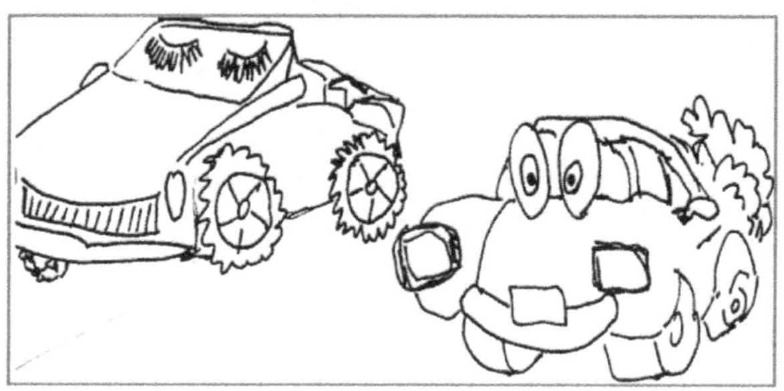

Once upon a time, there was a hardtop named Harry who lived a simple and routine life. Harry went to the gas station, filled his tank, drove around town and returned to the station when he ran low. This system worked pretty well as long as Harry remembered to check his gauges. All in all, Harry was a happy and well-maintained car.

One day, while finishing a routine fill up, Harry noticed a shiny new sports car at the next pump. What a beauty! Her sleek lines and glistening red body set his engine racing. He smiled at her shyly. As she pulled away, she called, "Catch me if you can."

Excited by the adventure, Harry dashed after her. He followed her up and down and all around town. The shiny new sports car traveled very fast and although Harry was only a few years old he had to huff and puff most of the time just to keep her in sight.

Every time Harry got within a foot or two of the shiny new sports car, she would give him a teasing laugh and dash quickly out of reach. Obsessed by the chase, Harry followed her for days and nights, forgetting all about resting or checking his gauges. No matter how fast Harry pushed himself, he couldn't seem to catch her.

One day, the shiny new sports car caught a stop-light. Harry couldn't believe his luck. He raced his engine madly and pulled up beside her. He was far too winded to speak, but he managed a big warm smile. The shiny new sports car swiped her wipers seductively. Harry's little engine flooded with joy.

The light changed and the shiny new sports car sped merrily away.

Harry stalled empty. Not only was he out of gas, but he had cracked his block in his herculean effort to make the light.

A very tired and sad Harry was towed to the repair shop for a complete and very expensive overhaul.

If we are chasing a goal that is breaking us down, do we focus past the winning to consider what we are losing?

Rethinking Fear Exercise H
Fear of Not Achieving a Goal

Harry was so intent on his goal that he ran himself to physical breakdown.

Maybe, like Harry, you are chasing a goal that is breaking you down? Maybe your goal has become an obsession? Maybe you are ignoring your health or your family or your finances? Maybe you are afraid to stop to tend to your needs for fear you won't achieve your goal?

What if you took a moment *right now* to begin to rethink your fear of not achieving your goal and observe how you have allowed this to affect your thinking and behavior? You can start by asking yourself the following questions.

Thoughts:
Is this the only goal I feel I can achieve?
Am I willing to create a Plan B to achieve this goal?
Am I willing to look at other options?
Do I understand I have a responsibility to myself to tend to my needs?
Am I willing to create a balanced life that allows me to meet my needs and goals?
Am I willing to ask for help when I need it?
Have I allowed myself to ignore my responsibilities to others by focusing so intently on this goal?
Do I need to rebuild friendships that I have ignored?
Your brain has power. What ideas come to mind on how you can resolve this fear? List them.

Emotions:
What am I afraid will happen if I don't achieve this goal?
Have I connected my self-worth to achieving this goal?
Am I feeling alone and unsupported due to isolating myself?
Am I feeling emotionally exhausted?
Do I want to practice the four W's (Who, When, Why, What) from the Value of Emotional Intelligence Chapter to help better define my emotions about my fear of not achieving this goal?
Your emotional and physical health are important. Are you suffering from depression or anxiety and need to speak with your doctor? Do you feel you could benefit from counseling? What steps do you need to take to seek help through services available to you? Take action now.

Life Impact:
How is my fear of not achieving this goal affecting:
My relationships?
My health?
My work?
My happiness?
Your life is your creation. Your thoughts, emotions and actions create reactions. What impact has your fear of not achieving a goal had on your life so far? Are you willing to make changes?

Moving Forward:
What kind of healthy neurotransmitter bridges did I build today?
Your new thoughts and emotions about your fear of not achieving a goal increased your neurotransmitters and created new "go to bridges" for you to use in the future. Continue improving your life.
Congratulate yourself for taking the action to rethink your fear! You are worth the effort!

Take a Break and Breathe:
Rethinking fear can be stressful, so don't overwhelm yourself.
Raise your hands in the air and stretch.
Take a deep breath.
Smile.
Take the dog for a walk.
Pet the cat.
Call a friend.
Eat a piece of chocolate.
Do something that relaxes you.
Step away from the book.

I

IVAN THE IMPERIOUS INSECT

Ivan was a handsome royal-purple insect who considered himself a powerful leader. Intimidation was his weapon of choice, for he believed the only way to keep his swarm in line was to be tough.

"Faster! Faster!" Ivan shouted. "Move, you idiots! Move!"

Although Ivan's title was a source of much pride, he found being the leader a frustrating job. Keeping the swarm together and moving forward drained his energy. Each night, he dragged himself home and flopped into his favorite chair, exhausted.

"They're slow and they're stupid," Ivan confided to his wife. "They sap my strength."

"Surely there must be one with basic intelligence. Perhaps you can train him to help so you won't be so tired," suggested his wife.

Over the next several days, Ivan studied the insects while they buzzed through their tasks. He saw that one insect with red wings moved along more confidently than the others. He decided he would honor this one with the privilege of taking on some of his duties.

"What is your name?" asked Ivan, approaching the insect with the red wings.

"Will," answered the insect.

Ivan gifted him with a wide grin. "Well, Will, today is your lucky day. I've decided to give you the honor of taking on some of my duties."

"No thanks," answered Will.

Ivan's smile twisted into an angry frown. "You ungrateful idiot! Do you realize I could have chosen any insect in the swarm? Any of them would die for an honor like this."

"I doubt it," replied Will. "Why would any of us want to help someone who intentionally demeans us?" And off Will flew.

When dealing with others, how often do we stop to consider what the experience is like from their side?

Rethinking Fear Exercise I
Fear of Others Not Listening

We can call Ivan a bad boss, but that would be minimizing his problem. Ivan didn't know how to be a boss. He didn't appreciate his swarm's talents and abilities. He was afraid his swarm wouldn't listen to him unless he acted like a tyrant.

Maybe, like Ivan, you have not learned the skills that would allow you to be a more positive boss, parent, spouse or friend? Maybe you are afraid that if you don't bark orders, others won't listen to you?

What if you took a moment *right now* to begin to rethink your fear of others not listening to you and observe how you have allowed this to affect your thinking and behavior? You can start by asking yourself the following questions.

Thoughts:
Why is it necessary for others to listen to me?
Is my way the only way to accomplish the task?
Could the task be accomplished if others did it their way?
Am I willing to educate myself about improving my communication skills?
Am I willing to stop micromanaging others and learn to respect their talents?
Am I willing to forego being a tyrant and incorporate a team concept?
Do I owe others apologies?
Do I need to rebuild relationships I have trashed?
Your brain has power. What ideas come to mind on how you can resolve this fear? List them.

Emotions:
How do I feel when someone does what I want?
Am I addicted to a "high" from the sense of power?
How do I feel when someone does not listen to me?
What fear is associated with my feelings?
Do I want to practice the four W's (Who, When, Why, What) from the Value of Emotional Intelligence Chapter to help better define my emotions about my fear of others not listening?
Your emotional and physical health are important. Are you suffering from depression or anxiety and need to speak with your doctor? Do you feel you could benefit from counseling? What steps do you need to take to seek help through services available to you? Take action now.

Life Impact:
How is my fear of others not listening affecting:
My relationships?
My health?
My work?
My happiness?
Your life is your creation. Your thoughts, emotions and actions create reactions. What impact has your fear of others not listening had on your life so far? Are you willing to make changes?

<table>
<tr><td>Moving Forward:</td></tr>
<tr><td>What kind of healthy neurotransmitter bridges did I build today?</td></tr>
<tr><td>Your new thoughts and emotions about your fear of others not listening increased your neurotransmitters and created new "go to bridges" for you to use in the future. Continue improving your life.</td></tr>
<tr><td>Congratulate yourself for taking the action to rethink your fear! You are worth the effort!</td></tr>
</table>

Take a Break and Breathe:
Rethinking fear can be stressful, so don't overwhelm yourself.
Raise your hands in the air and stretch.
Take a deep breath.
Smile.
Take the dog for a walk.
Pet the cat.
Call a friend.
Eat a piece of chocolate.
Do something that relaxes you.
Step away from the book.

J

JONATHON JUNKYARD

Jonathon Junkyard had a dream. He dreamed of being transformed.

He was tired of being lonely and dirty with broken refrigerators and bags of trash and rusted autos. He was tired of his nights being disturbed by drunken people shooting rats.

He dreamed of well-kept grass and a playground of swings and slides and teeter-totters. He dreamed of parents and children filling his yard with laughter.

Although Jonathon dreamed these things, he didn't really believe they would come true. But the dreaming helped him get through the misery of his days and not feel so depressed about his life. So he kept on dreaming his dream.

One day, big trucks and groups of adults and teens came to his junkyard. The trucks began to haul away the rusted autos and broken equipment. The adults and teens began removing the bags of trash and clearing away the loose debris.

Jonathon got very excited. He couldn't quite believe it was happening, but his dream was coming true. Today was the day he would become a playground. He had never felt this happy before. He could barely contain himself.

By day's end, Jonathon had been transformed from a haphazard junkyard to a neatly organized recycle center. He had bins for cardboard and bins for newspapers. He had bins for glass and bins for wood. He had bins for small electronics. He even had bins for clothing donations.

Jonathon waited until the last adult drove away and then he began to cry. All day, he had believed he was being transformed. He had believed his dream was coming true. But there would be no playground. There would be no laughter. He was nothing more than an elevated junkyard. Jonathon cried all night long from deep disappointment.

The next morning, an official sign was erected at Jonathon's entrance. The mayor arrived with a delegation. Reporters came to film the event. Speeches were made about how important the center was and how it would serve the community for many years. Everyone applauded and celebrated the new recycle center.

As Jonathon listened, he felt less alone. The community would be coming by regularly now. He was cleaner and more organized with an official sign and an official purpose. True, he hadn't been elevated to a playground like he had dreamed, but at least he wasn't a lonely junkyard anymore. Jonathon decided to join the celebration. After all, if he could become a recycle center today, he might still be transformed into a playground tomorrow.

If our dreams don't come true as expected, do we choose to suffer with disappointment or do we choose to celebrate where we are in the present?

Rethinking Fear Exercise J
Fear of Disappointment

Jonathon was able to turn his disappointment into celebrating the recycling center while still maintaining his dream of becoming a playground someday.

Maybe, like Jonathon, you have not attained your dream yet? Maybe you are feeling disappointed and frustrated? Maybe you are afraid you will never attain your dream?

What if you took a moment *right now* to begin to rethink your fear of disappointment and observe how you have allowed this to affect your thinking and behavior? You can start by asking yourself the following questions.

Thoughts:
Why is it necessary for me to attain this particular dream?
Do I understand that I already have worth and my dream won't make me more worthy?
Do I have a realistic plan for attaining my dream?
Am I willing to improve my talents, skills and abilities needed to attain my dream?
Am I willing to find a mentor to help me?
Am I willing to network with others in my desired field?
Am I willing to appreciate, find joy and celebrate where I am right now?
Your brain has power. What ideas come to mind on how you can resolve this fear? List them.

Emotions:
How do I feel when I picture myself attaining my dream?
Do I feel a sense of worth I don't feel now?
Does it make me feel better than others?
How do I feel when I think of never attaining my dream?
What feelings do I associate with failure?
Do I want to practice the four W's (Who, When, Why, What) from the Value of Emotional Intelligence Chapter to help better define my emotions about my fear of disappointment?
Your emotional and physical health are important. Are you suffering from depression or anxiety and need to speak with your doctor? Do you feel you could benefit from counseling? What steps do you need to take to seek help through services available to you? Take action now.

Life Impact:
How is my fear of disappointment affecting:
My relationships?
My health?
My work?
My happiness?
Your life is your creation. Your thoughts, emotions and actions create reactions. What impact has your fear of disappointment had on your life so far? Are you willing to make changes?

<table>
<tr><td>Moving Forward:</td></tr>
<tr><td>What kind of healthy neurotransmitter bridges did I build today?</td></tr>
<tr><td>Your new thoughts and emotions about your fear of disappointment increased your neurotransmitters and created new "go to bridges" for you to use in the future. Continue improving your life.</td></tr>
<tr><td>Congratulate yourself for taking the action to rethink your fear! You are worth the effort!</td></tr>
</table>

<table>
<tr><td>Take a Break and Breathe:</td></tr>
<tr><td>Rethinking fear can be stressful, so don't overwhelm yourself.</td></tr>
<tr><td>Raise your hands in the air and stretch.</td></tr>
<tr><td>Take a deep breath.</td></tr>
<tr><td>Smile.</td></tr>
<tr><td>Take the dog for a walk.</td></tr>
<tr><td>Pet the cat.</td></tr>
<tr><td>Call a friend.</td></tr>
<tr><td>Eat a piece of chocolate.</td></tr>
<tr><td>Do something that relaxes you.</td></tr>
<tr><td>Step away from the book.</td></tr>
</table>

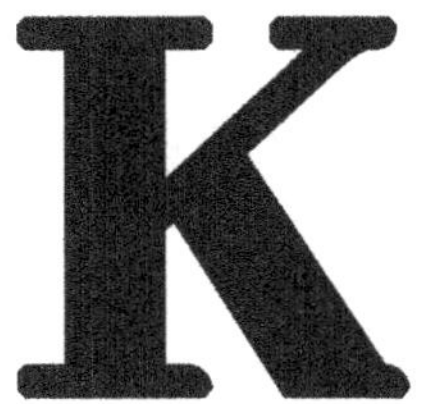

KATIE THE KILLER KITE

High in the sky flew a kite named Katie. Katie had long ago left her owner to float about freely. Bright yellow with pink fringe and an orange tail, she appeared rather garish, but appealing none-the-less.

Katie was a master at catching the slightest wind and loved soaring along at a fast pace. Her one failing was her bent for hitting into things. She got caught in trees, electric wires, roof-tops, but, luckily, someone always came along to free her and she'd take off again more or less unscathed.

One day, while sailing along at a pretty rapid speed, Katie collided with a blue jay. Katie was unhurt, but the blue jay had the wind knocked out of him and fell to the ground. Gliding fast and not wanting to stop, Katie assumed the blue jay would recover unharmed. Katie quite often ran into birds and all had recovered as far as she knew.

Two ravens flying nearby saw what happened and called out to Katie, "Is he all right?"

"I'm sure he's fine," replied Katie as she kept flying forward.

The ravens circled back and landed next to the blue jay. After examining him, the larger raven stated, "His neck is broken. He's dead."

After burying him and putting a twig cross on his grave, the ravens hurried to catch up with Katie.

"The blue jay is dead," the ravens informed Katie.

"Well, it's not my fault. It was an accident," excused Katie.

"Have you no remorse?" asked the ravens.

"It's not like I ran into him on purpose. I was flying freely. He should have seen me coming and turned away." And with that, Katie caught an incoming thermal and took off.

If our freedom clashes with another's, do both parties hold responsibility? Does one? Does none?

Rethinking Fear Exercise K
Fear of Taking Responsibility

Katie showed no remorse in the death of the blue jay. Although others had helped her out of trees and wires, she flew independently through life without stopping to help anyone, not even the blue jay who had fallen to the ground. She took no responsibility for her actions.

Maybe, like Katie, you fly freely though life only focused on your own interests? Maybe you have not learned to develop empathy? Maybe you don't notice or ignore others feelings and needs? Maybe you hurt others with your carelessness? Maybe you don't apologize for the pain you inflict? Maybe you are afraid to stop and take responsibility for your actions?

What if you took a moment *right now* to begin to rethink your fear of taking responsibility and observe how you have allowed this to affect your thinking and behavior? You can start by asking yourself the following questions.

Thoughts:
Why do I find it difficult to apologize when I have hurt someone?
Do I understand that taking responsibility is a sign of strength?
Am I willing to assess and improve my behavior?
Am I willing to respect the rights of others?
Am I willing to develop empathy?
Am I willing to apologize to those I have injured?
Your brain has power. What ideas come to mind on how you can resolve this fear? List them.

Emotions:
Why do I feel others don't matter?
What is the fear associated with my taking responsibility?
Do I feel a sense of entitlement over others?
Do I want to practice the four W's (Who, When, Why, What) from the Value of Emotional Intelligence Chapter to help better define my emotions about my fear of taking responsibility?
Your emotional and physical health are important. Are you suffering from depression or anxiety and need to speak with your doctor? Do you feel you could benefit from counseling? What steps do you need to take to seek help through services available to you? Take action now.

Life Impact:
How is my fear of taking responsibility affecting:
My relationships?
My health?
My work?
My happiness?
Your life is your creation. Your thoughts, emotions and actions create reactions. What impact has your fear of taking responsibility had on your life so far? Are you willing to make changes?

Moving Forward:
What kind of healthy neurotransmitter bridges did I build today?
Your new thoughts and emotions about your fear of taking responsibility increased your neurotransmitters and created new "go to bridges" for you to use in the future. Continue improving your life.
Congratulate yourself for taking the action to rethink your fear! You are worth the effort!

Take a Break and Breathe:
Rethinking fear can be stressful, so don't overwhelm yourself.
Raise your hands in the air and stretch.
Take a deep breath.
Smile.
Take the dog for a walk.
Pet the cat.
Call a friend.
Eat a piece of chocolate.
Do something that relaxes you.
Step away from the book.

LARRY THE LOAFER

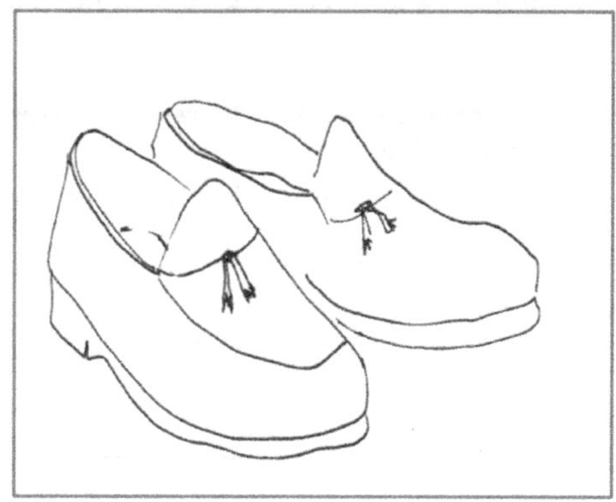

Larry was a smooth brown loafer with a tightly tied tassel. He was quite a good-looking shoe and held a prominent place in the display case.

Having a style very popular with the office set, Larry was purchased by the manager of the local downtown bank. Larry was very proud of having been chosen by someone of such high stature.

Every evening, the bank manager polished Larry to a gleaming shine. Larry called out to his other shoe friends as he walked through the town, "Hey, Ralph, do you see whose feet I'm on? Look how shiny he keeps me. Am I lucky or what?"

"Very nice," responded Ralph.

"Hey, Sally, still pinching the librarian's feet? She looks pretty uncomfortable," teased Larry.

Sally didn't reply.

"Hey, Clyde, you're pretty scuffed there. Hasn't your owner heard of polish?" Larry taunted.

Clyde lowered his eyes in embarrassment as his owner walked away.

For the next couple months, Larry enjoyed lauding his status over the other shoes. Tired of Larry's bragging, soon none of the other shoes bothered to speak to him. Larry didn't care. He liked feeling better than the others. It felt good being a step above the rest.   One day, the bank manager's daughter was playing with some glitter glue and accidently spilled it on her father's shoes. Larry expected to be cleaned and polished immediately. Instead he was thrown in the donation bin.

Larry felt humiliated at being discarded. His status was gone. Larry nervously wondered what would happen to him now.

If we derive our value from someone else's status, do we cease to exist when they leave us?

Rethinking Fear Exercise L
Fear of Having No Value

Larry used his owner's status to inflate his ego. From his aggrandized mindset, he made unkind statements to others. Because Larry connected his value to that of his owner, he had no value of his own making. Being thrown in the donation bin was shocking to Larry's sense of worth.

Maybe, like Larry, you have associated your value with your achievement, your work, your talents or your partner? Maybe you brag about it or laud it over others thinking it makes you sound important? Maybe you are afraid that without it, you have no worth?

What if you took a moment *right now* to begin to rethink your fear of having no value and observe how you have allowed this to affect your thinking and behavior? You can start by asking yourself the following questions.

Thoughts:
Do I understand that I have value simply because I exist?
Do I understand that trying to prove my worthiness exposes my lack of self-confidence?
Am I willing to stop bragging about my achievements, work, talents or partner to try to make myself seem valuable?
Am I willing to appreciate what I bring to my life?
Am I willing to take steps to build my self-confidence?
Am I willing to present myself to others as I am?
Your brain has power. What ideas come to mind on how you can resolve this fear? List them.

Emotions:
Why do I feel I have no value as myself?
What is the feeling I derive from bragging about my achievement, work, talents or partner?
Is there anything else I do that gives me this same feeling?
If I had no achievement, work, talents or partner to brag about, what would I feel?
Do I often feel empty inside?
Do I want to practice the four W's (Who, When, Why, What) from the Value of Emotional Intelligence Chapter to help better define my emotions about my fear of having no value?
Your emotional and physical health are important. Are you suffering from depression or anxiety and need to speak with your doctor? Do you feel you could benefit from counseling? What steps do you need to take to seek help through services available to you? Take action now.

Life Impact:
How is my fear of having no value affecting:
My relationships?
My health?
My work?
My happiness?
Your life is your creation. Your thoughts, emotions and actions create reactions. What impact has your fear of having no value had on your life so far? Are you willing to make changes?

Moving Forward:
What kind of healthy neurotransmitter bridges did I build today?
Your new thoughts and emotions about your fear of having no value increased your neurotransmitters and created new "go to bridges" for you to use in the future. Continue improving your life.
Congratulate yourself for taking the action to rethink your fear! You are worth the effort!

Take a Break and Breathe:
Rethinking fear can be stressful, so don't overwhelm yourself.
Raise your hands in the air and stretch.
Take a deep breath.
Smile.
Take the dog for a walk.
Pet the cat.
Call a friend.
Eat a piece of chocolate.
Do something that relaxes you.
Step away from the book.

THREE MERRY MARBLES

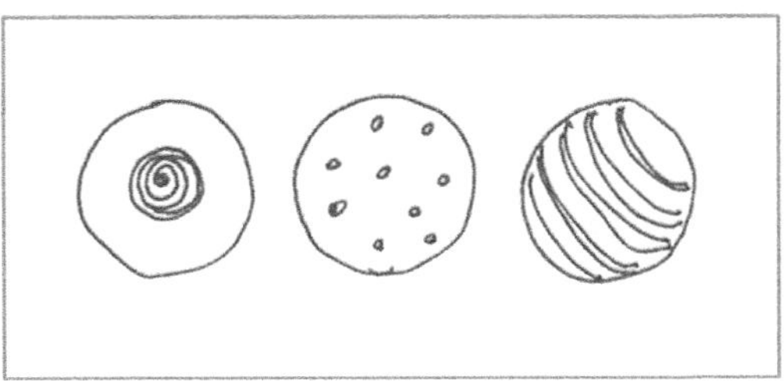

Three merry marbles sat in a row, basking in the bright morning sunlight.

The first marble was baby blue with a cherry-red center. The second marble was lime green with vibrant purple dots. The third marble was glittering gold with delicate white stripes.

All three waited proudly to be chosen for play.

Two children came by. Each chose a marble, leaving one.

The baby blue with a cherry-red center sat all alone.

"Why didn't either child want me? I'm attractive. I'm exceptionally skilled and never break the rules. Why didn't the children choose me? Maybe I wasn't friendly enough? Could I have offended one of them? I feel so sad and lonely." And the baby blue with a cherry-red center doubted himself and felt terribly rejected...all day long. And at day's end, when the children returned the other marbles, he hid his head in shame.

The next day, two children came by. Each chose a marble, leaving one.

The lime green with the vibrant purple dots sat all alone.

"How could this happen to me? I'm the perfect marble. The kids always pick me. Sometimes, they've even fought over me.

They've got some nerve turning on me this way. They won't get away with this. I'll show them. Tomorrow, I'm holding out. I'll refuse to play." And the lime green with the vibrant purple dots complained and felt angry…all day long. And at day's end, when the children returned the other marbles, he chastised them bitterly.

On the third day, two children came by. Each chose a marble, leaving one.

The glittering gold with the delicate white stripes sat all alone.

"I have to admit it kind of hurts my pride not to have been chosen. But, I'm not going to let it ruin my day. I've had my share of play-time. I've been rolled by the best and the worst. And tomorrow I'll probably be chosen again. Actually, it's kind of nice to have a day to just kick back and relax in the sun." And the glittering gold with the delicate white stripes basked in the sunlight and felt perfectly contented…all day long. And at day's end, when the children returned the other marbles, he asked them about their day and enjoyed hearing their stories.

If life gives us both wins and losses, do we choose to take both personally or do we choose to relax and find the enjoyment in each?

Rethinking Fear Exercise M
Fear of Rejection

The marbles' different responses are examples of their attachment to someone else's decision. The blue with the cherry-red center chose to be sad, the green with the purple dots chose to be angry, but the gold with the white stripes chose to relax and enjoy the day.

Maybe, like the blue with the cherry-red center, you become sad when someone doesn't include you or give you the attention you feel you deserve? Maybe, like the green with the purple dots, you become angry if someone doesn't act the way you expect or want? Maybe you go from happy to sad because your emotional response is dependent on others' actions? Maybe you view every action as acceptance or rejection?

What if you took a moment *right now* to begin to rethink your fear of rejection and observe how you have allowed this to affect your thinking and behavior? You can start by asking yourself the following questions.

Thoughts:
Do I understand that my reactions are my choice and have nothing to do with others?
Do I understand that I have complete control over my responses to situations?
Am I willing to stop taking others' actions personally?
Am I willing to separate myself from knee jerk reaction and realistically appraise a situation?
Am I willing to take responsibility for my responses?
Your brain has power. What ideas come to mind on how you can resolve this fear? List them.

Emotions:
Why do I feel everything is about me?
How often do I allow my mood to be influenced by others' actions?
What events trigger my feelings of rejection?
How do I respond when I feel rejected?
Do I display outbursts of anger?
Do I feel my emotions are out of my control?
Do I want to practice the four W's (Who, When, Why, What) from the Value of Emotional Intelligence Chapter to help better define my emotions about my fear of rejection?
Your emotional and physical health are important. Are you suffering from depression or anxiety and need to speak with your doctor? Do you feel you could benefit from counseling? What steps do you need to take to seek help through services available to you? Take action now.

Life Impact:
How is my fear of rejection affecting:
My relationships?
My health?
My work?
My happiness?
Your life is your creation. Your thoughts, emotions and actions create reactions. What impact has your fear of rejection had on your life so far? Are you willing to make changes?

Moving Forward:
What kind of healthy neurotransmitter bridges did I build today?
Your new thoughts and emotions about your fear of rejection increased your neurotransmitters and created new "go to bridges" for you to use in the future.   Continue improving your life.
Congratulate yourself for taking the action to rethink your fear! You are worth the effort!

Take a Break and Breathe:
Rethinking fear can be stressful, so don't overwhelm yourself.
Raise your hands in the air and stretch.
Take a deep breath.
Smile.
Take the dog for a walk.
Pet the cat.
Call a friend.
Eat a piece of chocolate.
Do something that relaxes you.
Step away from the book.

NICHOLAS THE NICKLE

All of the quarters, dimes, nickels and pennies arrived on time for the meeting except Nicholas. He was late as usual. The silver dollar, as main speaker, had just reached the podium when Nicholas came running in, out of breath and sweating profusely. He sat in the back hoping no one, especially his boss, Henry, had noticed he was late. Everyone, including Henry, had noticed.

When the meeting was over, his boss asked to speak with him privately. Nicholas knew he was in trouble and entered Henry's office with dismay.

"Well, Nicholas, what do you have to say?" asked Henry.

"I'm sorry, sir. I would have been on time, but I got lost in a coat pocket and by the time I got out I was running late."

"If I recall correctly, last week you were late because you got lost in a purse. And the week before, you fell out of a wallet. Do you recall what you promised when we met after that last occasion?"

"I said I would start out earlier so that if I ran into a problem I could still arrive on time."

"And did you?"

"No, sir."

"You will be given one last chance, Nicholas. If you are not on time at next week's meeting, you will be fired. Do you understand?"

"Yes, sir."

The next week, Nicholas arrived ten minutes early for the meeting. When he walked in, the meeting room was empty. No other nickels, pennies, dimes or quarters were present. Nicholas checked his calendar to make sure he had the correct date and time. He confirmed he was correct. He didn't understand where everyone else could be.

After about twenty minutes time, the others entered the room. Nicholas felt angry about having made an effort to be ten minutes early and then having to wait twenty minutes for the others. He eyed them crossly, but none apologized for being late. They acted as if it were perfectly all right to have kept Nicholas waiting.

Still angry after the meeting, Nicholas decided to speak with his boss. "Henry, I made a point of being ten minutes early and everyone else was twenty minutes late."

"You seem angry," stated Henry.

"I am. Their being late was inconsiderate."

"Why was it inconsiderate?"

"Well, it's like their time is more important than mine. It's like they don't think I'm as valuable."

"Perhaps you have a better idea now how we feel when you are late?"

If we consistently run late, does our time really warrant priority or are we simply inconsiderate of others?

Rethinking Fear Exercise N
Fear of Not Being in Control

Having often been the one who was late, Nicholas didn't realize what it felt like to be on the receiving end of that behavior until his coworkers kept him waiting.

Maybe, like Nicholas, you often run late? Maybe you assume that your family, friends or coworkers will wait for you? Maybe you are not aware of how inconsiderate your behavior seems to others? Maybe you are afraid that being on time lessens your control?

What if you took a moment *right now* to begin to rethink your fear of not being in control and observe how you have allowed this to affect your thinking and behavior? You can start by asking yourself the following questions.

Thoughts:
How often do I keep my family, friends and coworkers waiting?
What excuses do I use for my tardiness?
Do I consider my time more important than theirs?
Do I use being late as a way to control them?
Do I understand that my behavior is selfish and disrespectful?
Am I willing to take responsibility and improve my behavior?
Do I need to apologize to others?
Your brain has power. What ideas come to mind on how you can resolve this fear? List them.

Emotions:
Why do I feel everyone else should wait for me?
Do I use being late as a way to reassure myself that others will support me no matter how inconsiderate my behavior?
Do I feel a sense of power when others have to wait for me?
How do I feel when others comment on my being late?
Do I feel shame and guilt for bad behavior?
Do I feel angry that I'm being called on my behavior?
Do I want to practice the four W's (Who, When, Why, What) from the Value of Emotional Intelligence Chapter to help better define my emotions about my fear of not being in control?
Your emotional and physical health are important. Are you suffering from depression or anxiety and need to speak with your doctor? Do you feel you could benefit from counseling? What steps do you need to take to seek help through services available to you? Take action now.

Life Impact:
How is my fear of not being in control affecting:
My relationships?
My health?
My work?
My happiness?
Your life is your creation. Your thoughts, emotions and actions create reactions. What impact has your fear of not being in control had on your life so far? Are you willing to make changes?

Moving Forward:
What kind of healthy neurotransmitter bridges did I build today?
Your new thoughts and emotions about your fear of not being in control increased your neurotransmitters and created new "go to bridges" for you to use in the future. Continue improving your life.
Congratulate yourself for taking the action to rethink your fear! You are worth the effort!

Take a Break and Breathe:
Rethinking fear can be stressful, so don't overwhelm yourself.
Raise your hands in the air and stretch.
Take a deep breath.
Smile.
Take the dog for a walk.
Pet the cat.
Call a friend.
Eat a piece of chocolate.
Do something that relaxes you.
Step away from the book.

THE OLD ONE

Once upon a time, there was a small village at the foot of a beautiful mountain. The mountain air was crisp and clean and the full moon shone large and bright above it.

The local villagers followed the cycles of the moon and were particularly attached to the full moon. They gathered their crops during the time of the full moon. They held their galas during the time of the full moon. They made important decisions during the time of the full moon. The full moon brought them joy and peace of mind.

One particularly dark and cloudy month, the full moon was obscured from view night after night.

This worried the villagers and they began to talk among themselves and exchanged ideas. Their discussions only made them more fearful.

Someone suggested they gather at the home of the old one and ask her advice. The old one was much respected and known for her wise words of counsel.

"What does this mean?" one of the villagers asked the old one.

"Are we in danger?" asked another.

"Has the full moon disappeared forever?" asked a third.

"What if it never returns?" queried several.

"We are afraid!" cried the villagers.

"Fear not," advised the old one. "This situation is temporary. The full moon will rise again. There is nothing to fear. Calm yourselves. Go back to your homes. Go back to your work. Focus on your daily chores."

Knowing the old one always told the truth, the villagers sighed with relief, smiled at one another, shook hands all around and went back to their homes and their work.

"Mother," asked the old one's daughter after the crowd had dispersed, "what if the full moon doesn't return? Won't the villagers panic again?"

"They will adapt to the change," stated the old one confidently. "Once focus is drawn away from panic and back to living, the cause of the fear becomes nothing more than trivial inconvenience."

When we are paralyzed with fear, wouldn't it be helpful to remember we have the ability to refocus?

Rethinking Fear Exercise O
Fear of Change

When the old one refocused the villagers' attention on their daily chores, performing familiar actions helped calm their fears. The change in the moon was accepted as an event rather than a catastrophe.

Maybe, like the villagers, you panic at change? Maybe you find change difficult and allow yourself to become rattled? Maybe your fear of change causes you to make poor choices or unreasonable demands?

What if you took a moment *right now* to begin to rethink your fear of change and observe how you have allowed this to affect your thinking and behavior? You can start by asking yourself the following questions.

Thoughts:
Do I think of change as a catastrophe?
Do I try to control events and people to keep them from changing?
Do I understand I have the ability to accept change?
Do I understand that I am capable of taking care of myself no matter what the change?
Do I understand that accepting change and making a plan to deal with it will create a smoother transition?
Am I willing to seek advice and explore methods to help me cope with change?
Your brain has power. What ideas come to mind on how you can resolve this fear? List them.

Emotions:
What is it about change that frightens me?
Do I feel insecure or incapable of coping with something new or different?
Do I stress myself worrying that things might change?
Am I still holding emotion about major changes that have occurred in my past?
What are the emotions I am holding and feeling?
How did I respond to those major changes at the time they occurred?
Do I respond the same way to minor changes?
Do I want to practice the four W's (Who, When, Why, What) from the Value of Emotional Intelligence Chapter to help better define my emotions about my fear of change?
Your emotional and physical health are important. Are you suffering from depression or anxiety and need to speak with your doctor? Do you feel you could benefit from counseling? What steps do you need to take to seek help through services available to you? Take action now.

Life Impact:
How is my fear of change affecting:
My relationships?
My health?
My work?
My happiness?
Your life is your creation. Your thoughts, emotions and actions create reactions. What impact has your fear of change had on your life so far? Are you willing to make changes?

<table>
<tr><td>Moving Forward:</td></tr>
<tr><td>What kind of healthy neurotransmitter bridges did I build today?</td></tr>
<tr><td>Your new thoughts and emotions about your fear of change increased your neurotransmitters and created new "go to bridges" for you to use in the future. Continue improving your life.</td></tr>
<tr><td>Congratulate yourself for taking the action to rethink your fear! You are worth the effort!</td></tr>
</table>

<table>
<tr><td>Take a Break and Breathe:</td></tr>
<tr><td>Rethinking fear can be stressful, so don't overwhelm yourself.</td></tr>
<tr><td>Raise your hands in the air and stretch.</td></tr>
<tr><td>Take a deep breath.</td></tr>
<tr><td>Smile.</td></tr>
<tr><td>Take the dog for a walk.</td></tr>
<tr><td>Pet the cat.</td></tr>
<tr><td>Call a friend.</td></tr>
<tr><td>Eat a piece of chocolate.</td></tr>
<tr><td>Do something that relaxes you.</td></tr>
<tr><td>Step away from the book.</td></tr>
</table>

P

PATRICIA THE PARROT TULIP

Winter had exited, but the ground was far from thawed. Spring was not yet visible. None of the flowers were willing to risk the cold, hard surface above them.

Anxious to be announced, Spring called all of the crocuses, lilies, daffodils and tulips to a conference to see if she could find a willing volunteer.

Patricia the parrot tulip was teaming with inner excitement and indecision. Her intuition urged her to volunteer, but her head shouted fear of the cold, hard ground. Nevertheless, she took a deep breath, followed her heart and stepped forward. The other flowers applauded her courage with sighed relief.

"I am very grateful," announced Spring, "but you are so delicate and fail to bloom even under the best conditions. Perhaps you should reconsider."

"All the reason why I must go," answered Patricia. "If I fail to bloom, you can attribute it to my delicate disposition. But if I do survive, as I am sure I will, think how grand and rare the announcement will be. In either case, Spring will not lose face and the rest of the flowers will have gained time for softer entrances."

Spring assented and Patricia the parrot tulip began to inch her way slowly to the surface.

"You're moving too slowly," noted a crocus. "You should burst up and open very quickly, staying close to the ground."

"No, no," disagreed a lily. "You should hold your bloom tightly closed until warmer weather."

"You won't burst through," interjected a daffodil. "Parrot tulips are known for suffocating as the ground warms."

But the icy ground kept Patricia cool and she bloomed that year and every year thereafter. By following her instincts, she had discovered her key to survival.

If our intuition reveals our best opportunities for growth, do we move forward bravely or do we surrender to the fears of others?

Rethinking Fear Exercise P
Fear of Following Intuition

Patricia followed her intuition and it was the key to her success. She didn't allow the other flowers' fears to keep her from moving forward.

Maybe, like Patricia, your intuition is pushing you to take some action? Maybe your family or friends are against you doing it? Maybe you are afraid they might be right or afraid they may reject you and have not allowed yourself to move forward?

What if you took a moment *right now* to begin to rethink your fear of following your intuition and observe how you have allowed this to affect your thinking and behavior? You can start by asking yourself the following questions.

Thoughts:
What in my life is my intuition pushing me to address?
Have I considered the pros and cons for taking this action?
Do I have a backup plan if this doesn't work out?
Do I understand that my life is mine to live and I am responsible to myself for my choices?
Am I willing to follow the path that is best for me?
Your brain has power. What ideas come to mind on how you can resolve this fear? List them.

Emotions:
What do I feel when I imagine myself following my intuition?
Why do I allow others to hold me back?
Do I feel they have a right to do so?
Do I dread their disapproval?
Am I afraid they will reprimand, yell at or leave me?
What feelings come over me when I think of their possible reaction?
Do I feel brave enough to move forward with what I know is best for me?
Do I have an emotional support group if I choose to do so?
Do I want to practice the four W's (Who, When, Why, What) from the Value of Emotional Intelligence Chapter to help better define my emotions about my fear of following my intuition?
Your emotional and physical health are important. Are you suffering from depression or anxiety and need to speak with your doctor? Do you feel you could benefit from counseling? What steps do you need to take to seek help through services available to you? Take action now.

Life Impact:
How is my fear of following my intuition affecting:
My relationships?
My health?
My work?
My happiness?
Your life is your creation. Your thoughts, emotions and actions create reactions. What impact has your fear of following your intuition had on your life so far? Are you willing to make changes?

Moving Forward:
What kind of healthy neurotransmitter bridges did I build today?
Your new thoughts and emotions about your fear of following your intuition increased your neurotransmitters and created new "go to bridges" for you to use in the future. Continue improving your life.
Congratulate yourself for taking the action to rethink your fear! You are worth the effort!

Take a Break and Breathe:
Rethinking fear can be stressful, so don't overwhelm yourself.
Raise your hands in the air and stretch.
Take a deep breath.
Smile.
Take the dog for a walk.
Pet the cat.
Call a friend.
Eat a piece of chocolate.
Do something that relaxes you.
Step away from the book.

THE QUIVERING QUETZAL

Deep in the forest of Central America lived a young quetzal named Henrico. Even by the most relaxed quetzal standards, his looks were most inadequate. He had none of the brilliant red or bronze-green plumage. He possessed no long flowing tail feathers. His color was lackluster brown and his tail feathers resembled limp fringe.

The other birds taunted and teased him so unmercifully that Henrico often quivered with fear. Escaping to his hiding spot high up in the trees, he calmed his shaking and reflected on his ugliness. He couldn't understand why he was born so different from the others. He viewed himself a freak of nature. Feeling defective and defenseless, Henrico suffered in isolation.

Henrico's mother, Generosa, frequently uttered words of encouragement, but neither her words nor her unconditional love seemed to soothe his pain.

One day while sitting alone, Generosa sighed and shook her head with worry. "What will become of my poor Henrico?"

"Don't worry so," spoke a voice from above.

She looked up sharply. On the limb above her sat her old, faded and partially bald great-uncle. "Great-Uncle, I thought you died years ago!" she exclaimed in surprise.

"No. Still alive. Here to pay a visit. Be gone again soon," answered Great-Uncle in short, snappy spurts.

"Come. Join us for dinner," suggested Generosa warmly. "I will invite the relatives and we will celebrate your visit." And off she flew to prepare.

All through dinner, Henrico squealed with delight as Great-Uncle recited exciting stories of his many journeys. Generosa doubted most were true, but so happy was she to see Henrico smile, she encouraged Great-Uncle on.

After dinner, Henrico and Great-Uncle went flying. For the first time in his young life, Henrico allowed his insecurities to fall, spread his wings with pride and soared free and happy next to Great-Uncle.

Before long the other birds gathered 'round and began their usual taunts. Henrico allowed their words to crush his spirit. Darting from Great-Uncle's side, he quickly flew to the top of his tallest hiding tree. Once there, he sobbed bitterly, quivering in fear and shame.

"What a view you have here," complimented Great-Uncle as he settled himself on a branch beside Henrico.

Henrico quickly wiped the tears from his face and looked down at the lush greenery and sparkling waterfall below. "I've never noticed the beauty. I'm always thinking sad thoughts when I run from them." Henrico motioned to the birds circling below.

"Why let them bother you?"

"What they say is true. I *am* ugly," answered Henrico sadly.

Great-Uncle studied him for a long moment. "Are you embarrassed by me?"

"No, Great-Uncle," stated Henrico sincerely.

"I'm a lot uglier than you. Bald and faded. Got torn feathers, too."

"But that does not matter. You are special. You have had adventures," praised Henrico.

"Yep. Had many adventures. Couldn't have had them hidden in a tree. Do you think?"

"No, Great-Uncle," smiled Henrico.

What would happen if we rejected the limitations of social standards and proudly chose to spread our unique wings?

Rethinking Fear Exercise Q
Fear of Ridicule

Henrico allowed the other birds' comments about his looks to affect his self-esteem. He became so withdrawn that he failed to notice the beautiful view from his favorite hiding place. Great-Uncle helped Henrico to understand that looks have nothing to do with his right to a full life of wonderful adventures.

Maybe, like Henrico, you have allowed others' comments to lessen your enjoyment of life? Maybe you have allowed others to humiliate you? Maybe you have been hiding your talents and abilities? Maybe you are reluctant to explore your life for fear others will make fun of you?

What if you took a moment *right now* to begin to rethink your fear of ridicule and observe how you have allowed this to affect your thinking and behavior? You can start by asking yourself the following questions.

Thoughts:
What is a hurtful thing someone has said to me that I keep repeating to myself?
Do I consider it a true fact or only their opinion?
Why do I allow what others say to affect my choices?
Do I understand that I have every right to enjoy my life as I am?
Am I willing to take actions that encourage my confidence in myself?
Am I willing to live my life ignoring those who try to hinder my joy?
Am I willing to appreciate my talents and abilities?
Your brain has power. What ideas come to mind on how you can resolve this fear? List them.

Emotions:
What do I feel when someone makes a hurtful comment to or about me?
How do I react when someone makes a hurtful comment to or about me?
Do I allow others hurtful comments to ruin my day, week, month, year or future?
Do I ride an on-going roller coaster powered by the positive and negative comments from others?
Do I feel unable to control my emotions?
Do I want to practice the four W's (Who, When, Why, What) from the Value of Emotional Intelligence Chapter to help better define my emotions about my fear of ridicule?
Your emotional and physical health are important. Are you suffering from depression or anxiety and need to speak with your doctor? Do you feel you could benefit from counseling? What steps do you need to take to seek help through services available to you? Take action now.

Life Impact:
How is my fear of ridicule affecting:
My relationships?
My health?
My work?
My happiness?
Your life is your creation. Your thoughts, emotions and actions create reactions. What impact has your fear of ridicule had on your life so far? Are you willing to make changes?

<table>
<tr><td>

Moving Forward:

What kind of healthy neurotransmitter bridges did I build today?

Your new thoughts and emotions about your fear of ridicule increased your neurotransmitters and created new "go to bridges" for you to use in the future. Continue improving your life.

Congratulate yourself for taking the action to rethink your fear! You are worth the effort!

</td></tr>
</table>

<table>
<tr><td>

Take a Break and Breathe:

Rethinking fear can be stressful, so don't overwhelm yourself.

Raise your hands in the air and stretch.

Take a deep breath.

Smile.

Take the dog for a walk.

Pet the cat.

Call a friend.

Eat a piece of chocolate.

Do something that relaxes you.

Step away from the book.

</td></tr>
</table>

RITA THE RAGING RABBIT

Rita the rabbit thumped in rage…often. Everyone knew not to cross her, but it was hard to tell what would upset her. Sometimes, just saying, "Good morning, Rita," would set her off.

Eventually, tired of tirades, Rita's husband, Randy, left her. And, contrary to custom, took the litter with him. His note said he was sorry but he couldn't take the stress of living with her and couldn't trust her alone with the kittens. All were heading off to make new, and much calmer, lives for themselves.

Naturally, Rita did not take this calmly and thumped so loudly she cracked the walls of the burrow. Although she felt hurt and wanted to cry, she was too furious to allow the tears.

Feeling the need to complain to someone, Rita called her best friend, Helen. Truth be told, Helen was Rita's only friend. Rita's other friends, tired of being abused, had dropped her.

"Can you believe that selfish buck left me?" complained Rita to Helen. "And he convinced those sniveling kittens to go with him. Well, I don't need any of them."

"I'm very sorry," replied Helen.

"You're sorry? That's it. Your sympathy doesn't pay my bills. What's it matter to you? You've got a massive warren. I'm going to have to work two jobs now just to maintain mine."

"I don't know what you want me say," offered Helen.

"Some friend you are!" shouted Rita.

Although Helen felt sad that Rita was suffering, she perfectly understood why Randy and the kittens needed a break from Rita's impossible temper.

"Rita, do you think if you offered to get some counseling, Randy and the kittens would come back?" asked Helen cautiously.

"Counseling? Counseling for what?"

"Counseling for your temper, Rita," suggested Helen.

"I have every right to have a temper. I had a lousy kittenhood and a miserable life ever since. It's not fair!" complained Rita.

"But you are not a kitten now, Rita. You have control over how you act as a doe," offered Helen.

If we learned from our past and moved forward, maybe we could stop inflicting our suffering on others?

Rethinking Fear Exercise R
Fear of Examining Anger

Rita had unresolved anger about something she had experienced as a kitten. Rather than address her anger and resolve it, Rita forced her anger onto others in unhealthy ways.

Maybe, like Rita, you have unresolved anger about something that you experienced in the past? Maybe your anger causes discord with family or friends or gets you into trouble on the job? Maybe you don't intend to get angry but your anger feels overwhelming and you feel you must release it or explode? Maybe you use your anger to cover the pain you feel inside? Maybe you feel your anger is all that keeps you from falling apart? Maybe you are not even sure why you are angry? Maybe you are afraid to examine your anger?

What if you took a moment *right now* to begin to rethink your fear of examining your anger and observe how you have allowed this to affect your thinking and behavior? You can start by asking yourself the following questions.

Thoughts:
What events happened in the past that caused this anger issue?
Who was there?
What did they say?
What did I say?
Do I understand that I do not need to continue to carry these events and anger issues?
Am I willing to take responsibility for resolving my anger issues?
Am I willing to learn how to express my anger in a healthy way?
Your brain has power. What ideas come to mind on how you can resolve this fear? List them.

Emotions:
What triggers an angry response from me?
Does it happen with only certain people or only at certain instances? List them.
What do these people or instances have in common?
Is this commonality similar to past events that hurt me?
Was I able to express my anger at that time?
If not, what would I say to express my anger about it now?
Do I feel overwhelmed by my feelings of anger and pain?
Do I feel unable to examine my anger on my own and need counseling to help me?
Do I have no idea why I am angry and need outside help to provide insight?
Do I want to practice the four W's (Who, When, Why, What) from the Value of Emotional Intelligence Chapter to help better define my emotions about my fear of examining my anger?
Your emotional and physical health are important. Are you suffering from depression or anxiety and need to speak with your doctor? Do you feel you could benefit from counseling? What steps do you need to take to seek help through services available to you? Take action now.

Life Impact:
How is my fear of examining my anger affecting:
My relationships?
My health?
My work?
My happiness?
Your life is your creation. Your thoughts, emotions and actions create reactions. What impact has your fear of examining your anger had on your life so far? Are you willing to make changes?

<table>
<tr><td>Moving Forward:</td></tr>
<tr><td>What kind of healthy neurotransmitter bridges did I build today?</td></tr>
<tr><td>Your new thoughts and emotions about your fear of examining your anger increased your neurotransmitters and created new "go to bridges" for you to use in the future. Continue improving your life.</td></tr>
<tr><td>Congratulate yourself for taking the action to rethink your fear! You are worth the effort!</td></tr>
</table>

<table>
<tr><td>Take a Break and Breathe:</td></tr>
<tr><td>Rethinking fear can be stressful, so don't overwhelm yourself.</td></tr>
<tr><td>Raise your hands in the air and stretch.</td></tr>
<tr><td>Take a deep breath.</td></tr>
<tr><td>Smile.</td></tr>
<tr><td>Take the dog for a walk.</td></tr>
<tr><td>Pet the cat.</td></tr>
<tr><td>Call a friend.</td></tr>
<tr><td>Eat a piece of chocolate.</td></tr>
<tr><td>Do something that relaxes you.</td></tr>
<tr><td>Step away from the book.</td></tr>
</table>

S

STEWART THE SILLY SEAGULL

Acting silly and entertaining the other seagulls brought Stewart great pleasure.

One blustery, stormy day when the seagulls huddled together on shore to ride out the storm, Stewart couldn't resist the large audience. He left the colony and flew high into the air. He tossed about in the current, dove deep into the sea catching fish and flew high in the air dropping them in the mouths of his audience. The laughter of the other seagulls encouraged him to fly farther out to sea where the stronger current helped increase his antics.

Suddenly, Stewart swirled out of control and plopped into the sea in a graceless manner. The impact bruised Stewart's body and caused his head to ache, but after a few minutes, Stewart rallied and slowly flew back to the shore.

Most of the seagulls applauded his safe return, but Stewart felt shamed by the snickers of some of the others. The rest of the day, he lay low and quietly kept to himself.

Over the next few weeks, whenever Stewart had the urge to entertain, he remembered those snickers from his fellow seagulls and was afraid to soar for fear something embarrassing would happen.

Months passed with Stewart shying away from the group and denying himself those old joyful feelings of entertaining.

Eventually, Stewart moved to another shore and found a new flock of seagulls to entertain. His exuberant personality returned and Stewart was living a happy life again.

One day, Stewart had just returned from a lively high dive act when he noticed one of the seagulls from his old flock talking to the seagulls in his new flock. Old feelings of shame flooded him and he flew away quickly to start a new life once again.

Is it better to spend energy carrying our shame from shore to shore or is it better to forgive our faults and set ourselves free?

Rethinking Fear Exercise S
Fear of Resolving Shame

Stewart allowed one embarrassing event to set him on a path of running and hiding for the rest of his life. No matter where he traveled, there was no guarantee that someone from his past would not show up and expose his shame. He would never be free.

Maybe, like Stewart, you have been carrying the shame of an unfortunate incident? Maybe you have gone to great lengths to protect your secret? Maybe you have sacrificed your integrity by embellishing the truth or changing details about your past? Maybe you are overcome with fear from time to time that someone will find out? Maybe you are afraid that if someone you love found out, they would reject you? Maybe you are trapped in a life of lies?

What if you took a moment *right now* to begin to rethink your fear of resolving the shame and observe how you have allowed this to affect your thinking and behavior? You can start by asking yourself the following questions.

Thoughts:
What is the shame I am hiding? Speak it aloud.
Did anyone witness the event that causes me this shame?
If so, what did they say or do?
What did I say and do at the time of the event?
Do I need to make amends for something I have done wrong?
If I make amends, am I willing to let go of my shame?
If I have no amends to make, am I willing to let go of my shame?
Your brain has power. What ideas come to mind on how you can resolve this fear? List them.

Emotions:
Why do I feel shame?
Am I carrying this shame to punish myself?
Why do I feel I need to punish myself?
What is the fear associated with resolving this shame?
Is this fear imagined or are there actual consequences to resolving my shame?
What are the consequences? List them.
Does it feel safe for me to disclose my shame to a trusted friend?
What is my fear of disclosing to this friend?
What do I need to do to make it safe for me to resolve my shame?
Do I want to practice the four W's (Who, When, Why, What) from the Value of Emotional Intelligence Chapter to help better define my emotions about my fear of resolving my shame?
Your emotional and physical health are important. Are you suffering from depression or anxiety and need to speak with your doctor? Do you feel you could benefit from counseling? What steps do you need to take to seek help through services available to you? Take action now.

Life Impact:
How is my fear of resolving my shame affecting:
My relationships?
My health?
My work?
My happiness?
Your life is your creation. Your thoughts, emotions and actions create reactions. What impact has your fear of resolving your shame had on your life so far? Are you willing to make changes?

Moving Forward:
What kind of healthy neurotransmitter bridges did I build today?
Your new thoughts and emotions about your fear of resolving your shame increased your neurotransmitters and created new "go to bridges" for you to use in the future. Continue improving your life.
Congratulate yourself for taking the action to rethink your fear! You are worth the effort!

Take a Break and Breathe:
Rethinking fear can be stressful, so don't overwhelm yourself.
Raise your hands in the air and stretch.
Take a deep breath.
Smile.
Take the dog for a walk.
Pet the cat.
Call a friend.
Eat a piece of chocolate.
Do something that relaxes you.
Step away from the book.

T

TIPURA THE TROUBLED TIGER

Long ago, in a remote jungle of East India, lived a great tiger named Tipura. His striping was of the highest contrast, reflecting beautifully in the sunlight. His coat was thick as the richest rug. He provided well for his family, was a fine competitor and had true reason to proudly pace the jungle.

As the years passed and Tipura grew older, his coat grew thinner and lost some of its luster. Every time Tipura noticed these changes, he growled angrily and fiercely at the young male tigers. His actions stemmed from fear, for deep inside he worried about his ability to still compete. The maturing males were becoming as wonderfully strong and beautiful as he had once been. Growing older made him feel inadequate and frightened.

One night, Tipura had a dream that he challenged all the young males to a competition. Instead of them quaking in fear, they laughed at his challenge and his tired old body. Startled awake, he related his dream to his wife, Triska, who snuggled closely and reassuringly as he spoke.

"How am I to compete?" asked Tipura. "I am growing too old to challenge these sturdy young males. My dream means that I am no longer useful."

"Perhaps," said Triska, "your dream means only that it is time to change? Maybe it is a sign to use your abilities in a different way?"

"But I have always been the strongest," stated Tipura proudly. "Now," he sighed, "I am growing old and inferior."

"Perhaps age is a reminder that competition alone no longer offers us lessons?" suggested Triska. "Perhaps age is a signal to share what we have learned? Tipura, with your many great qualities, no one can make you inferior. Do not allow jealousy, insecurity and fear to destroy all that you are."

Tipura appreciated Triska's insights and thanked her with a kiss.

The next day, Tipura set about restoring his spirit, his mind and his body to a fuller sense of purpose. He replaced his fragile outer ego with strong inner worth. He walked the jungle securely, offering help wherever needed.

And because of his willingness to share his knowledge, the young male tigers looked to him as their leader, sought his counsel and praised him publicly.

If Pythagoras was right and the age of wisdom begins at 55, do we share that knowledge or do we refuse to grow wise?

Rethinking Fear Exercise T
Fear of Getting Older

Tipura was able to change his fear of growing older to a more lasting sense of purpose. Rather than focus on staying young, he embraced the knowledge he had gleaned over the years and shared his wisdom through mentoring others.

Maybe, like Tipura, you have insecurities about growing older? Maybe you have become obsessed with comparing yourself to those who are younger? Maybe you feel insecure about your wrinkles or your hairline? Maybe you feel you must spend time, energy and money to prove you have not aged? Maybe you feel getting older means you are no longer vital? Maybe you are ashamed of your age and try to hide it from others? Maybe you associate aging with death?

What if you took a moment *right now* to begin to rethink your fear of getting older and observe how you have allowed this to affect your thinking and behavior? You can start by asking yourself the following questions.

Thoughts:
Do I understand that my age is simply a number and does not define my vitality, intellect or creativity?
Do I understand that my process of growing older is unique to me?
Am I willing to celebrate my talents, abilities and lessons learned?
Am I willing to share my knowledge and experience with others?
Am I willing to experience the joy of life no matter what my age?
Your brain has power. What ideas come to mind on how you can resolve this fear? List them.

Emotions:
What is my greatest fear about getting older?
Is that fear real or imagined?
Am I allowing others opinions about age to frighten me?
When I picture myself older, what feelings come over me?
Am I afraid as I get older someone will reject me?
Is this true or imagined?
Am I willing to speak to this person about my fear of rejection?
Do I want to practice the four W's (Who, When, Why, What) from the Value of Emotional Intelligence Chapter to help better define my emotions about my fear of getting older?
Your emotional and physical health are important. Are you suffering from depression or anxiety and need to speak with your doctor? Do you feel you could benefit from counseling? What steps do you need to take to seek help through services available to you? Take action now.

Life Impact:
How is my fear of getting older affecting:
My relationships?
My health?
My work?
My happiness?
Your life is your creation. Your thoughts, emotions and actions create reactions. What impact has your fear of getting older had on your life so far? Are you willing to make changes?

Moving Forward:
What kind of healthy neurotransmitter bridges did I build today?
Your new thoughts and emotions about your fear of getting older increased your neurotransmitters and created new "go to bridges" for you to use in the future. Continue improving your life.
Congratulate yourself for taking the action to rethink your fear! You are worth the effort!

Take a Break and Breathe:
Rethinking fear can be stressful, so don't overwhelm yourself.
Raise your hands in the air and stretch.
Take a deep breath.
Smile.
Take the dog for a walk.
Pet the cat.
Call a friend.
Eat a piece of chocolate.
Do something that relaxes you.
Step away from the book.

U

URSULA THE UNHAPPY UMBRELLA

Unmarried and desperately longing for a soul-mate to complete her, Ursula cried often. Luckily, she lived in a stormy state so her tears were often mistaken for raindrops.

Ursula's tight-knit group of friends all suffered woes. One had a terrible boss who treated him mean. One had a selfish husband who left her home alone. Another had two spoiled children who drove her to distraction. And the last had a sickly relative he resented doting upon.

The group met weekly to complain to one another about the people who made their lives miserable. Swapping stories briefly reduced their pain, but then they returned to their sad lives and the unhappiness resumed. Occasionally, one would make an effort toward change, but it was usually half-hearted and short-lived.

Ursula, on the other hand, made many efforts to find her soul-mate. She was an active participant in twenty-two dating sites. She went on many first dates, for she was very attractive, but had few second or third dates. She couldn't understand why since she had tried her best to be exactly what they wanted. Still, none had been interested in committing to a long-term relationship and marriage.

Willing to try anything for a loving, useful life, Ursula read the latest books on dating, met with the most popular psychics and covered her mirrors with positive affirmations. None of it worked and the deep rejection she felt lowered her self-esteem.

One day, Ursula ran into her old college friend, Alice. Ursula tried her best to avoid Alice because inevitably old friends asked if she was married and she had to hold back tears when she responded she was not. But Alice pursued her and the brief conversation pleasantly resulted in plans for lunch.

Lunch was filled with laughter, talk of mutual friends and reminiscences of old classmates. Although neither spoke of marriage, Ursula noticed that Alice was not wearing a wedding band either and assumed they suffered mutually.

As their friendship renewed, Alice invited Ursula to many charity events and community group activities. Ursula found one of the causes particularly important to her and became a chairperson, donating much time to fundraising efforts.

Over the next year, Ursula spent much less time with her group of woe and much more time giving to others. She stopped looking for a soul-mate to complete her and began living an active, happy and complete life of her own.

And she hardly ever cried.

If we think about how to spend the years allotted us, do we wait to become useful tomorrow or do we create a useful life today?

Rethinking Fear Exercise U
Fear of Loneliness

By involving herself in community activities, Ursula became focused on purpose and started living her life. She stopped trying to find someone to complete her and recognized she could be complete on her own. She realized life had meaning with or without a mate.

Maybe, like Ursula, you have been waiting to start your life? Maybe you have become obsessed with having a relationship to be happy? Maybe you feel a sense of rejection, insecurity or unfairness at being alone? Maybe you are lonely? Maybe you feel unhappy? Maybe you feel unloved? Maybe you associate having a relationship with self-worth? Maybe you fear a life of loneliness?

What if you took a moment *right now* to begin to rethink your fear of loneliness and observe how you have allowed this to affect your thinking and behavior? You can start by asking yourself the following questions.

Thoughts:
Do I understand that being alone is not the same as being lonely?
How do I spend my free time? Make a list.
Do I participate in events that bring me joy?
Do I believe I have value on my own?
Do I have at least one purposeful focus in my life?
What are my talents? Make a list.
Am I willing to share them with a charity, group or business?
Am I willing to attend an uplifting event this week?
Am I willing to create a purposeful and happy life for myself?
Your brain has power. What ideas come to mind on how you can resolve this fear? List them.

Emotions:
What fear arises about my not having a relationship?
Do my friends reinforce my fear?
Do I feel hurt if someone makes a comment about my being alone?
Do I wallow in my loneliness?
Do I feel defective or worthless because I am alone?
Do I have someone in my life who supports me for who I am?
How do I feel when I am with that person?
Do I want to practice the four W's (Who, When, Why, What) from the Value of Emotional Intelligence Chapter to help better define my emotions about my fear of loneliness?
Your emotional and physical health are important. Are you suffering from depression or anxiety and need to speak with your doctor? Do you feel you could benefit from counseling? What steps do you need to take to seek help through services available to you? Take action now.

Life Impact:
How is my fear of loneliness affecting:
My relationships?
My health?
My work?
My happiness?
Your life is your creation. Your thoughts, emotions and actions create reactions. What impact has your fear of loneliness had on your life so far? Are you willing to make changes?

Moving Forward:
What kind of healthy neurotransmitter bridges did I build today?
Your new thoughts and emotions about your fear of loneliness increased your neurotransmitters and created new "go to bridges" for you to use in the future. Continue improving your life.
Congratulate yourself for taking the action to rethink your fear! You are worth the effort!

Take a Break and Breathe:
Rethinking fear can be stressful, so don't overwhelm yourself.
Raise your hands in the air and stretch.
Take a deep breath.
Smile.
Take the dog for a walk.
Pet the cat.
Call a friend.
Eat a piece of chocolate.
Do something that relaxes you.
Step away from the book.

V

THE VALIANT LITTLE VIOLET

Once upon a time there was a little violet growing happily within a bright sunflower patch. The little violet loved his shaded spot, content to be dwarfed by the yellow giants surrounding him.

Every day, the giant sunflowers filtered the rays of the noon-day sun so that the little violet could be fed without being wilted. In return, the little violet provided soothing words to the giant sunflowers when their large yellow heads were picked upon by birds or whipped about by stiff winds.

One day, the young girl who owned the bright sunflower patch spotted the little violet. She fell in love with the delicate blossoms and proudly invited her friends to come see him. Everyone "oohed" and "aahed" at his beauty and the young girl was much pleased.

"Oh, little violet," said the young girl, "you're so lovely. It's sad that you are so tiny and hidden in the greenery. I wish you were large like the sunflowers. Then I could gaze at you from my window."

In a valiant effort to please the young girl, the little violet pushed the protective greenery aside to absorb more sun-light and stretched his roots in hopes of growing taller. Soon, the additional sun faded the little violet's flowers and the stretching created tears in his roots. Eventually, the little violet withered and died.

Shortly afterward, when the young girl was walking past the bright sunflower patch, she noticed the dead little violet. She gently pulled up the wilted remnant and felt sad, remembering how lovely it had been.

If our desire is to please others, do we destroy ourselves fulfilling their whims or do we choose to gift them with our authentic selves?

Rethinking Fear Exercise V
Fear of Being Yourself

In a desire to grow tall to please the young girl, the little violet tried to change his nature and destroyed his life.

Maybe, like the little violet, you have been trying to change your nature to please someone? Maybe someone criticizes your looks, personality, talents or interests and you feel shamed into changing? Maybe you have different ideas from your family or friends and feel obligated to go along with a way of life that is not comfortable for you? Maybe you are trying to make yourself into a different person to gain the affection of someone who doesn't accept you as you are? Maybe you are a people pleaser and trying to be everything to everyone? Maybe you are afraid of being yourself for fear of rejection?

What if you took a moment *right now* to begin to rethink your fear of being yourself and observe how you have allowed this to affect your thinking and behavior? You can start by asking yourself the following questions.

Thoughts:
What is it I think I have to change about myself?
Is someone asking me to change who I am?
What reason have they given for not accepting me as I am?
Is this change in accord with my integrity and responsibility to my own happiness?
Do I understand that I am deserving of love for the person I am right now?
Do I understand that I have the right to live my life according to my beliefs?
Am I willing to celebrate myself as I am with my current successes and failures?
Am I willing to strengthen my belief in myself?
Your brain has power. What ideas come to mind on how you can resolve this fear? List them.

Emotions:
How does it feel to not be accepted for who I am?
Am I feeling pressure to change myself?
Am I feeling like who I am as a person is not good enough?
Am I feeling rejected by someone I love?
What emotions surface for me when I'm with this person?
Do I feel I have someone in my life who accepts me for who I am?
How do I feel when I'm around this person?
Do I want to practice the four W's (Who, When, Why, What) from the Value of Emotional Intelligence Chapter to help better define my emotions about my fear of being myself?
Your emotional and physical health are important. Are you suffering from depression or anxiety and need to speak with your doctor? Do you feel you could benefit from counseling? What steps do you need to take to seek help through services available to you? Take action now.

Life Impact:
How is my fear of being myself affecting:
My relationships?
My health?
My work?
My happiness?
Your life is your creation. Your thoughts, emotions and actions create reactions. What impact has your fear of being yourself had on your life so far? Are you willing to make changes?

Moving Forward:
What kind of healthy neurotransmitter bridges did I build today?
Your new thoughts and emotions about your fear of being yourself increased your neurotransmitters and created new "go to bridges" for you to use in the future. Continue improving your life.
Congratulate yourself for taking the action to rethink your fear! You are worth the effort!

Take a Break and Breathe:
Rethinking fear can be stressful, so don't overwhelm yourself.
Raise your hands in the air and stretch.
Take a deep breath.
Smile.
Take the dog for a walk.
Pet the cat.
Call a friend.
Eat a piece of chocolate.
Do something that relaxes you.
Step away from the book.

THE WHIRLWIND AND THE WIZARD

In a land all too near was a Whirlwind who rushed about in constant motion. He had a very busy schedule. Many people to see. Many places to go. Many things to complete.

The Whirlwind was a firm believer in multi-tasking. He could juggle twelve projects before breakfast, attend six meetings before lunch and review eight contracts before dinner. Numerous were the completed items he checked off his "to do" lists.

One day, while attending a seminar on Type A personalities, the Whirlwind was introduced to the keynote speaker, the Wizard. After a brief but amicable exchange, the Whirlwind assessed the Wizard as an unrealistic fellow content with living off the laurels from an over-acclaimed time-management seminar.

The Wizard, on the other hand, found the brief encounter with the Whirlwind amusing. And although he felt the Whirlwind could benefit from a good dose of behavior modification, he thoroughly enjoyed meeting him.

Years later, quite by chance, the two met again.

"Nice to see you," greeted the Wizard. "Lovely flowers you have there?"

"Flowers? What? Oh yes, these. They asked me to present them to that recipient over there for some achievement or other."

"How have you been?" asked the Wizard.

"Very busy, very busy. Many projects going simultaneously. I can't begin to tell you how exhausting it is," stated the Whirlwind officiously. "And you?"

"Very happy, very happy. Thoroughly absorbed in a few projects at a time. I can't begin to tell you how joyful it is," replied the Wizard smiling.

If constant movement is our way of life, do we consider the expended time rewarding or merely time spent?

Rethinking Fear Exercise W

Fear of Slowing Down

The Whirlwind's constant motion kept him busy, but exhausted. Not only didn't he stop to smell the roses, he was barely aware they existed.

Maybe, like the Whirlwind, you run on a hectic schedule? Maybe you take on too many projects because you don't want to disappoint anyone? Maybe you handle everything yourself because you don't trust anyone to do it exactly like you? Maybe you refuse to take vacations to safeguard your job? Maybe you choose to keep moving so as not to deal with your feelings? Maybe you are afraid if you slowed down you might feel those feelings you keep at bay?

What if you took a moment right now to begin to rethink your fear of slowing down and observe how you have allowed this to affect your thinking and behavior? You can start by asking yourself the following questions.

Thoughts:
Am I willing to examine how I spend my time and reassess my commitments?
Am I willing to learn to say "No" to allow time for myself?
Am I willing to delegate tasks so I can slow down?
Am I willing to take time to feel and breathe and let go?
Am I willing to create moments of peace in my life?
Am I willing to deal with emotions that might surface?
Your brain has power. What ideas come to mind on how you can resolve this fear? List them.

Emotions:
What am I afraid will happen if I slow down?
What emotions surface when I am not busy?
Am I trying to numb those feelings with activity?
Are there any moments in my day when I feel safe? List them.
In those moments, am I alone or with someone?
Why do those moments feel safe?
Do I want to create more of those moments?
Do I want to practice the four W's (Who, When, Why, What) from the Value of Emotional Intelligence Chapter to help better define my emotions about my fear of slowing down?
Your emotional and physical health are important. Are you suffering from depression or anxiety and need to speak with your doctor? Do you feel you could benefit from counseling? What steps do you need to take to seek help through services available to you? Take action now.

Life Impact:
How is my fear of slowing down affecting:
My relationships?
My health?
My work?
My happiness?
Your life is your creation. Your thoughts, emotions and actions create reactions. What impact has your fear of slowing down had on your life so far? Are you willing to make changes?

Moving Forward:
What kind of healthy neurotransmitter bridges did I build today?
Your new thoughts and emotions about your fear of slowing down increased your neurotransmitters and created new "go to bridges" for you to use in the future. Continue improving your life.
Congratulate yourself for taking the action to rethink your fear! You are worth the effort!

Take a Break and Breathe:
Rethinking fear can be stressful, so don't overwhelm yourself.
Raise your hands in the air and stretch.
Take a deep breath.
Smile.
Take the dog for a walk.
Pet the cat.
Call a friend.
Eat a piece of chocolate.
Do something that relaxes you.
Step away from the book.

X

A XYRIS NAMED XENA

Although Xena's petite yellow flowers and grassy leaves often attracted admirers, her spiky personality soon drove them away. This left Xena with no close friends and only a few distant acquaintances.

Her motto of "reject them before they can reject me" resulted from Xena's fear of abandonment. She had been hurt once and was afraid of being hurt again.

Secretly, Xena yearned for friends with whom she could laugh and play, but her fears were too strong to allow anyone close.

One day a strong wind from the west blew a cactus into the field. He rolled 'round and 'round, laughing wildly.

Xena was intrigued with the strange plant's antics. His form was most unusual. She was particularly impressed with his sharp golden spines. She wished she had spines that sharp. Dangerous spines like that could protect her from being hurt.

With a final wild whirl, the cactus dug into the soil beside Xena and immediately took root.

"Oh, you startled me!" exclaimed Xena.

"Sorry," the cactus replied.

"Well, keep your distance," ordered Xena.

"Okay. Okay. Don't get nervous."

"Humpf," replied Xena.

"Guess since we're neighbors now, I should introduce myself. I'm Cholla Cactus, friends call me Teddy Bear."

"Is that some sort of joke?" asked Xena.

"Oh, don't be misled by my sharp spines. I'm really quite a companionable guy. Back home, the cactus wrens build their nests all over me. My spines secure their nests so they don't blow away in the hot, dry winds. They love me."

"Well, this isn't the Wild West, so keep your frightful spines to yourself," warned Xena.

"You've no need to fear me," soothed Teddy Bear.

"Just the same, stay away."

"What's your name?" asked Teddy Bear.

"My name is Xena. Why do you want to know?"

"Just being neighborly," replied Teddy Bear.

"Well, keep to yourself."

"I must say, Xena, you are a most welcoming neighbor," complimented Teddy Bear.

"What?"

Teddy Bear burst into laughter. So genuine was his outburst that Xena herself began to laugh.

"That's better," said Teddy Bear. "Tell me, Xena, why are you so afraid of me? I promise I won't hurt you."

"I've heard that before and I'm not buying it," replied Xena.

"Oh, so it's not just me, then. I get it. Someone hurt you once and now you won't allow yourself to trust anyone."

"I have every right to protect myself," haughtily stated Xena.

"Of course, you do. But being afraid of everyone is a pretty lonely way to live, don't you think?" asked Teddy Bear.

If putting up barriers makes us feel safe, are we protecting ourselves from pain or isolating ourselves from the experiences of life?

Rethinking Fear Exercise X

Fear of Getting Hurt

Xena's fear of being hurt again caused her put up a barrier to friendship. That barrier became more than protection; it isolated Xena. It resulted in her living a friendless life.

Maybe, like Xena, you were hurt once and are afraid to trust again? Maybe you use criticism to keep others away? Maybe you use silence to separate yourself from others? Maybe you obsess about others' words or actions looking for negative motives? Maybe you choose friends who bore you or who you can easily control to make yourself feel safe? Maybe you demand guarantees where no such guarantees exit? Maybe you view love as being unsafe? Maybe you equate vulnerability with weakness?

What if you took a moment *right now* to begin to rethink your fear of getting hurt and observe how you have allowed this to affect your thinking and behavior? You can start by asking yourself the following questions.

Thoughts:
Why do I assume I will get hurt if I allow someone close?
How many times have I been hurt in the past? Count them.
What were the circumstances in each case? Note them.
What were the similarities? Note them.
How did I contribute to my getting hurt?
Am I willing to examine my inability to recognize unsafe people?
Am I willing to learn to be more discriminating with my friendship?
Am I willing to respect myself and require others respect me as well?
Am I willing to take the time necessary to allow relationships to grow healthily?
Am I willing to deal with behaviors I need to change?
Am I willing to gift myself with the joy of loving relationships?
Your brain has power. What ideas come to mind on how you can resolve this fear? List them.

Emotions:
How did I feel when someone hurt me?
Am I still feeling those feelings as if they just happened?
Why am I continuing to inflict that hurt on myself?
What emotional fulfillment do I get from feeling that hurt?
Am I using my pain as an excuse for pity?
Do I think of myself as emotionally needy?
Do I think I am not worthy of love?
Do I want to practice the four W's (Who, When, Why, What) from the Value of Emotional Intelligence Chapter to help better define my emotions about my fear of getting hurt?
Your emotional and physical health are important. Are you suffering from depression or anxiety and need to speak with your doctor? Do you feel you could benefit from counseling? What steps do you need to take to seek help through services available to you? Take action now.

Life Impact:
How is my fear of getting hurt affecting:
My relationships?
My health?
My work?
My happiness?
Your life is your creation. Your thoughts, emotions and actions create reactions. What impact has your fear of getting hurt had on your life so far? Are you willing to make changes?

Moving Forward:
What kind of healthy neurotransmitter bridges did I build today?
Your new thoughts and emotions about your fear of getting hurt increased your neurotransmitters and created new "go to bridges" for you to use in the future. Continue improving your life.
Congratulate yourself for taking the action to rethink your fear! You are worth the effort!

Take a Break and Breathe:
Rethinking fear can be stressful, so don't overwhelm yourself.
Raise your hands in the air and stretch.
Take a deep breath.
Smile.
Take the dog for a walk.
Pet the cat.
Call a friend.
Eat a piece of chocolate.
Do something that relaxes you.
Step away from the book.

Y

YANCY THE YUPPY YAK

Yancy was an intelligent enough yak. He had a pleasing personality, made a good income and had a number of friends. His main problem was his indecisiveness.

Oh, he could easily decide between Russian and French dressing. He preferred French. And he could choose between buying a blue or grey suit. He bought the blue. But more important decisions were a challenge for him.

For example, should he take Sally or Shirley to the company picnic? Sally was much prettier, but she was a flirt. What if she came on to his boss or coworkers and embarrassed him? He trusted Shirley to be more professional, but she was plain and wouldn't elicit the type of envy he wanted to generate. Yancy struggled between the two until the day of the picnic. Unable to make a decision, he attended the picnic alone.

Choosing his new car was another exasperating example. Should he get the one with the best mileage rating or the one with the more comfortable seats? He had a fair commute to work so saving on gas would benefit his wallet, but he had a bad back so the more comfortable seats would benefit his health. Unable to make a decision on the new car, Yancy continued to drive his old clunker, which hurt his pocketbook and his back.

Although Yancy was an expert at organizing "pro" and "con" lists, he worried so about making a wrong choice that he studied them until his head hurt from exhaustion. On the rare occasions when he actually made a choice, he often wished he had chosen the alternative.

One day, Yancy's boss asked him to purchase new furniture for the conference room. As he usually did when making purchases, Yancy researched all of the options. He narrowed the choices to two, but couldn't decide which to buy. The oblong table would give them plenty of room for their meetings, but the round table would allow them to converse more easily.

Yancy questioned himself for weeks about which to choose. What if his boss didn't like the table he chose? What if his coworkers complained about the table? What if the table didn't hold up and they thought he wasted company funds? What if…?

And, as usual, Yancy continued to stress himself, afraid to make any decision at all.

Maybe if we eliminated judging our choices, we would stop paralyzing our lives with indecision and actually start living?

Rethinking Fear Exercise Y
Fear of Making Decisions

Yancy's fear of making the wrong choice created unneeded stress and proved detrimental to his health and happiness.

Maybe, like Yancy, you have a hard time making decisions? Maybe you don't research well enough to make informed decisions? Maybe you research so widely you confuse yourself with too many choices? Maybe you second guess yourself when you do reach a decision? Maybe you defer to others as a way of not making decisions? Maybe you can't accept possibly making a mistake? Maybe you lack confidence in your ability to make decisions? Maybe you are afraid others will mock you for the decisions you make?

What if you took a moment *right now* to begin to rethink your fear of making decisions and observe how you have allowed this to affect your thinking and behavior? You can start by asking yourself the following questions.

Thoughts:
Who mocked or reprimanded me about a previous decision I made?
What were the circumstances?
Do I think they had a right to do that?
Do I understand that I do not need to be perfect?
Do I understand that I do not need to justify my decisions to others?
Do I understand that I can change my mind if I don't like my first choice?
Am I willing to improve my decision making skills?
Am I willing to allow myself to make a snap decision and let go of the outcome?
Am I willing to play with and enjoy the options life provides me?
Your brain has power. What ideas come to mind on how you can resolve this fear? List them.

Emotions:
What am I afraid will happen if I make the wrong decisions?
Do I feel a decision I make cannot be undone?
Do I feel that I have to be perfect? Why?
Am I more afraid to make a decision around certain people?
Why do I feel afraid around those people and not others?
Have I ever made a mistake I felt okay about?
What made that mistake okay?
Do I want to practice the four W's (Who, When, Why, What) from the Value of Emotional Intelligence Chapter to help better define my emotions about my fear of making decisions?
Your emotional and physical health are important. Are you suffering from depression or anxiety and need to speak with your doctor? Do you feel you could benefit from counseling? What steps do you need to take to seek help through services available to you? Take action now.

Life Impact:
How is my fear of making decisions affecting:
My relationships?
My health?
My work?
My happiness?
Your life is your creation. Your thoughts, emotions and actions create reactions. What impact has your fear of making decisions had on your life so far? Are you willing to make changes?

Moving Forward:
What kind of healthy neurotransmitter bridges did I build today?
Your new thoughts and emotions about your fear of making decisions increased your neurotransmitters and created new "go to bridges" for you to use in the future. Continue improving your life.
Congratulate yourself for taking the action to rethink your fear! You are worth the effort!

Take a Break and Breathe:
Rethinking fear can be stressful, so don't overwhelm yourself.
Raise your hands in the air and stretch.
Take a deep breath.
Smile.
Take the dog for a walk.
Pet the cat.
Call a friend.
Eat a piece of chocolate.
Do something that relaxes you.
Step away from the book.

Z

THE ZUZTZ AND THE ZEEZEE

Once upon a time when the Earth was mostly water, there lived a group of Zuztzes who traveled about in canoes. This was a very dangerous task as the Earth was covered with dense fog and the Zuztzes could only see as far ahead as the tips of their canoes. Nevertheless, they fearlessly journeyed forward one stroke at a time.

One day a Zeezee bird flying high in the sky spun out on a thermal and accidentally toppled into the canoe of a Zuztz.

"Excuse the intrusion," apologized the Zeezee. "Sorry to disturb. I'll be off now," he said, flapping his wings. "Oh! I seem to have ruffled my wing. Just a kink, luckily," stated the Zeezee, examining it further. "Mind if I rest here a moment until it feels better?"

The Zuztz did not answer. He kept his eyes focused on his task. With each rhythmic stroke of his oar, he uttered a steady, "Ooooo."

The Zeezee bird studied the Zuztz for a moment. "You seem an awfully serious creature, all purpose and direction. How can you see where you're going in this fog?" questioned the Zeezee, suddenly realizing he was confined to this canoe until his wing healed. Used to flying above the fog, fear overcame him. "Do you even know your direction? What if you're traveling in circles? What if there's a giant rock ahead? What if you crash your canoe and sink?"

The Zuztz's eyes remained focused ahead. His only response was "Ooooo" as he paddled steadily forward.

"Look, you seem a strong and intelligent creature," complimented the Zeezee, trying a different approach. "Why would you concentrate so thoroughly on a paddle movement yet ignore all the possible dangers ahead? Surely you're not blind to this situation?'

"I am blind only to your useless fear," stated the Zuztz, carefully not missing one measured stroke.

"Fear? I'm not afraid. I'm cautious," countered the Zeezee. "You can't see where you're going. Have you thought of all the dangers that might be up ahead?"

"If I spend my time imagining dangers that may never be, who will paddle my canoe?" asked the Zuztz.

If fear of the future consumes us, do we forfeit the progress of today or do we move steadily forward with hope?

Rethinking Fear Exercise Z

Fear of the Future

While the Zuztz was moving his life forward one stroke at a time, the Zeezee bird was fearful of not being able to see what was ahead.

Maybe, like the Zeezee, you worry about what events might be ahead in your life? Maybe you deem the future too risky? Maybe you decline long-term plans in case something unforeseen happens? Maybe you deny yourself vacations lest something happen at home while you are away? Maybe you are reluctant to marry in case it does not work out? Maybe you settle for the same foods, activities or profession because you might not like something new? Maybe you have a fear of the future?

What if you took a moment *right now* to begin to rethink your fear of the future and observe how you have allowed this to affect your thinking and behavior? You can start by asking yourself the following questions.

Thoughts:
Do I understand there is no script for life?
Do I understand that life is the ultimate adventure?
Do I understand that life provides opportunities to explore and learn?
Do I understand that hiding under my bed cannot keep me safe?
Do I understand I have the skills and abilities to face my future?
Am I willing to continue to improve my skills to meet life's challenges?
Am I willing to move forward even when I'm frightened?
Your brain has power. What ideas come to mind on how you can resolve this fear? List them.

Emotions:
What is it about the future that frightens me?
Do I feel a need to control others and my environment?
Do I feel incapable of dealing with events in life?
Am I comfortable only in a set routine?
Do I fear making commitments?
Am I brave enough to poke my head out from under my bed?
Am I brave enough to change one thing in my set routine?
Am I brave enough to make and keep one small commitment?
Am I brave enough to try something I've never done before?
Do I want to practice the four W's (Who, When, Why, What) from the Value of Emotional Intelligence Chapter to help better define my emotions about my fear of the future?
Your emotional and physical health are important. Are you suffering from depression or anxiety and need to speak with your doctor? Do you feel you could benefit from counseling? What steps do you need to take to seek help through services available to you? Take action now.

Life Impact:
How is my fear of the future affecting:
My relationships?
My health?
My work?
My happiness?
Your life is your creation. Your thoughts, emotions and actions create reactions. What impact has your fear of the future had on your life so far? Are you willing to make changes?

Moving Forward:
What kind of healthy neurotransmitter bridges did I build today?
Your new thoughts and emotions about your fear of the future increased your neurotransmitters and created new "go to bridges" for you to use in the future. Continue improving your life.
Congratulate yourself for taking the action to rethink your fear! You are worth the effort!

Take a Break and Breathe:
Rethinking fear can be stressful, so don't overwhelm yourself.
Raise your hands in the air and stretch.
Take a deep breath.
Smile.
Take the dog for a walk.
Pet the cat.
Call a friend.
Eat a piece of chocolate.
Do something that relaxes you.
Step away from the book.

FINAL THOUGHTS

Discovering, learning, creating and growing are life-long processes that can provide you an adventurous understanding of yourself.

Rethinking your fear will not magically eliminate fear overnight. It takes time to change patterns we have developed over a life time.

Use the book as a reference. Whenever old fears resurface, engage in a mini review of a few of the questions in the book. Each time you do this, new insights will emerge and you will reinforce those "go to bridges" that you have already established.

As you continue your process of rethinking fear, you can employ the following truths we outlined in the Introduction as mantras to strengthen your dedication to moving forward:

- Your brain is your power supply
- You are accountable for your life choices
- Your happiness is solely your responsibility
- Your integrity shouts your worth
- Your momentum in life is dependent upon your response to change
- You have the right to ask for help without shame
- You *are* worth the effort

Your life is yours to live. What you do with it is up to you. I wish you happiness and success.

Exercise Your Power

Expand Your Brain

Stand Strong

Take Action

Enjoy Life

Made in the USA
Monee, IL
07 July 2026

56551629R00089